California Treasures

Practice Book

 Macmillan/McGraw-Hill

The *McGraw·Hill* Companies

**Mc
Graw
Hill** **Macmillan
McGraw-Hill**

Published by Macmillan/McGraw-Hill, of McGraw-Hill Education, a division of The McGraw-Hill Companies, Inc.,
Two Penn Plaza, New York, New York 10121.

Printed in the United States of America

9 10 HES 12

Contents

Unit 1 • Our Stories

Contents

Unit 2 • Ancient Civilizations

Contents

Unit 3 • A Question of Values

Contents

Unit 4 • Achieving Dreams

Contents

Unit 5 • Our Incredible Earth

Contents

Unit 6 • Rescue 9-1-1

Short vowel sounds are often spelled using just the vowel itself. For example, the letter *u* stands for the /u/ sound in *bug*, *cut*, and *nun*. The letter *i* stands for the /i/ sound in *big*, *kick*, and *lid*. Sometimes short vowel sounds have different spellings. For example, the /u/ sound is spelled by the *ou* in *trouble* and the *o* in *shove*. The short /e/ sound can be spelled by the *ea* in *thread*.

A. Read the word in the left column. Then circle the words on the right that make the same short vowel sound using a different spelling.

1. rug   bone   done   through   shove   over   double   money   though

2. din   rhythm   encyclopedia   pretty   very   myth   women

3. let   fiend   friend   said   laid   haystack   says   thread   head

B. Choose five of the words above that have the short vowel sound in them. Write a sentence for each word you chose. Underline the word you chose in each sentence.

4. _____

_____

5. _____

_____

6. _____

_____

7. _____

_____

8. _____

_____

Name _____

A. Write each vocabulary word next to its definition.

embarked	promenade	unimaginable	sensational
extravagant	lamented	precarious	establishment

1. expressed regret _____

2. not thinkable _____

3. leisurely walk _____

4. started out _____

5. arousing an intense interest _____

6. characterized by a lack of stability _____

7. a business or residence _____

8. extremely elaborate _____

B. Choose two vocabulary words. Use them in sentences of your own. Then draw a picture in the box below to illustrate one of your sentences.

9. _____

_____

10. _____

_____

 R 1.0 Word Analysis, Fluency, and Systematic Vocabulary Development

Name _____

Read the passage and answer the questions.

"Joshua, are you writing again?" asked Mrs. Talbot for what seemed like the hundredth time. "If you don't come down and participate in life, you aren't going to have anything to write about!"

Joshua didn't agree. He spent lots of time living. But he also spent lots of time writing. He recorded what happened during the school day, during breakfast, during dinner, and during playtime with friends. But in his writing, all the things happened on Mars set hundreds of years before or after they actually happened. It seemed to him that his life was much more interesting when he put it somewhere else in time or space. After all, Joshua planned on being a writer when he grew up. He needed lots of practice.

1. How does Joshua's mother feel about his writing?

   _____

2. What kind of writing does Joshua do? _____

   _____

   _____

   _____

3. Why does Joshua write stories about everything that happens to him?

   _____

4. How does Joshua feel about his life? _____

   _____

   _____

Write a short paragraph about your life as if it were set in another place and time. Use another sheet of paper if you need to.

   _____

   _____

   _____

   _____

© Macmillan/McGraw-Hill

Name _____

**As you read *Nothing Ever Happens on 90th Street,* fill in the
Conclusions Chart.**

What I Know	Text Evidence	Conclusions

How does the information you wrote in this Conclusions Chart help you
monitor comprehension of *Nothing Ever Happens on 90th Street*?

© Macmillan/McGraw-Hill

CA R 2.0 Reading Comprehension (Focus on Informational Materials)

Name _____

As I read, I will pay attention to punctuation.

	September 15, 3:41 P.M.
2	Hello, Peter Smith of Portland, Oregon. This is Julie Taylor
12	of Monterey, California. You may wonder why I'm writing
21	to you, since we don't know each other. It's because my entire
33	class is abuzz. Everybody is talking about Mr. Mora's big
43	announcement today. Mr. Mora is my teacher. Well, not just
53	mine, of course, but he's the teacher for our whole class.
64	My school is called Old Monterey Middle School, which is
74	a boring name. I would have called it the Monterey School
85	for Future Writers and Other Geniuses.
91	Mr. Mora laughed when I told him that. He said, "Well,
102	Julie, that name is a bit long, don't you agree?"
112	Mr. Mora is always asking us if we agree. Most of the
124	time I do. Mr. Mora knows a lot, especially about writing—
135	which brings me to the exciting announcement.
142	"Settle down, please," said Mr. Mora. It was almost three
152	o'clock, and we were getting restless. "I'm going to give you
163	a homework assignment—with a twist." 169

Comprehension Check

1. How do you think Peter Smith will respond? **Draw Conclusions**

2. How can you tell that Julie is a creative thinker? **Make Inferences**

	Words Read	–	Number of Errors	=	Words Correct Score
First Read		–		=	
Second Read		–		=	

CA R 1.1 Read aloud narrative and expository text fluently and accurately and with appropriate pacing, intonation, and expression.

When you interview a person, your purpose is to get specific information from her or him. Use the following guidelines for interviewing:

- Write your questions before the interview. Be sure to avoid questions that can be answered with a *yes* or a *no* answer.
- At the beginning of the interview, state your purpose directly.
- Remember that your job is to listen, not talk, during the interview.
- Listen closely to the responses, taking brief notes. If possible, tape-record the interview so you can revisit the information later. Be sure to get permission to tape.
- Ask follow-up questions to get more information or clarification about a topic.
- Immediately after the interview, review your notes and add information so you don't forget it later.

Suppose that you are preparing to interview your favorite author. You can focus the interview on his or her life, profession, a specific book, or another issue. Write a clear statement of your purpose. Then write five questions that will help you gather that information.

Purpose: _____

_____

1. _____

2. _____

_____

3. _____

_____

4. _____

_____

5. _____

_____

© Macmillan/McGraw-Hill

R 2.1 Identify the structural features of popular media (e.g., newspapers, magazines, online information) and use the features to obtain information.

Dictionaries provide readers with the histories of words as well as their meanings. The word's **origin** usually follows the pronunciation key and the identification of it as a part of speech. If you don't understand the abbreviations in the entry, check the front of the dictionary for a guide to the abbreviations. Some common ones are ME for Middle English, OE for Old English, F for French, L for Latin, and Gk for Greek.

Example: **describe** (di skrīb´) *vt* **described**; **describing** [ME, from L *describere*, from *de-* + *scribere* to write] 1. to give an account in words

A. Use a dictionary to find the origins of the words below. Record the earliest origin listed in the dictionary.

1. wrong: _____

2. scissors: _____

3. health: _____

4. govern: _____

5. split: _____

B. Use each of the words above in a sentence.

6. _____

_____

7. _____

_____

8. _____

_____

9. _____

_____

10. _____

_____

© Macmillan/McGraw-Hill

Name _____

Using the Word Study Steps

1. LOOK at the word.
2. SAY the word aloud.
3. STUDY the letters in the word.
4. WRITE the word.
5. CHECK the word.
   Did you spell the word right?
   If not, go back to step 1.

A. Find Rhyming Words

Circle the word in each row that rhymes with the spelling word on the left.

1. drill	drink	still	swell
2. threat	pet	treat	three
3. rank	rant	blank	rink
4. shrunk	shriek	rung	trunk
5. fund	run	stunned	funk
6. gram	grant	cram	train
7. dense	fence	dentist	ease
8. mock	stick	moist	lock
9. plaid	pleat	said	glad
10. clash	splash	class	juice

B. Write a poem of at least 4 lines. Include two of the spelling words in your poem.

_____

_____

_____

_____

© Macmillan/McGraw-Hill

LC 1.5 Spell frequently misspelled words correctly
(e.g., *their, they're, there*).

Name _____

A. Proofreading Activity

There are five spelling mistakes in this story. Circle the misspelled words. Write the words correctly on the lines below.

At midnight, I awoke to find the rain outside dripping in through my bedroom window. I put on my plade bathrobe and walked outside to see if I could stop it. I was surprised to see that the land around my house was covered in dence fog. As I was trying to prodd the window closed, I thought of the thret of being stranded in my house alone for days. This scared me so much that I forgot about the window and ran back into my house, full of dred.

1. _____
2. _____
3. _____
4. _____
5. _____

B. Writing Activity

Scary experiences can be fun to read about or write about. Do you like to read about such adventures? Write about a scary adventure. Use five spelling words in your writing.

_____
_____
_____
_____
_____
_____
_____
_____

 LC 1.5 Spell frequently misspelled words correctly
(e.g., *their, they're, there*).

Nothing Ever Happens on
90th Street • Grade 6/Unit 1   17

Name _____

> • An **imperative sentence** gives a command or makes a
>   request. It ends with a period.
> • An **exclamatory sentence** expresses strong feeling. It ends
>   with an exclamation point.

**A. Read each sentence. Write whether it is *declarative,
interrogative, imperative,* or *exclamatory*.**

1. What a wonderful camping trip that was!

   _____

2. Think about what Peter said about staying safe on a hike.

   _____

3. How many times have you climbed in the Shawangunk Mountains?

   _____

4. Don't delay getting down the mountain before sunset.

   _____

5. Richard couldn't decide whether or not to go.

   _____

6. I'm so excited to be on this hike!

   _____

**B. Revise the first four sentences. Change them to either
interrogative or declarative sentences.**

7. _____

8. _____

   _____

9. _____

   _____

10. _____

   _____

© Macmillan/McGraw-Hill

 LC 1.0 Written and Oral English Language Conventions

Name _____

- Begin a new sentence with a capital letter.
- **Declarative sentences** and **imperative sentences** end with a period.
- **Interrogative sentences** end with a question mark.
- **Exclamatory sentences** end with an exclamation point.

Rewrite the passage, correcting all capitalization and punctuation mistakes.

   i am so happy that rescue teams are on alert at all times to come to the aid of stranded or lost hikers i recently attended one of the classes teams hold to help campers think ahead about unexpected situations what if someone in my group became ill or injured what kind of weather conditions might I expect do I have the skills necessary to safely complete the trip I plan to make these questions never occurred to me

_____

_____

_____

_____

_____

_____

_____

_____

_____

© Macmillan/McGraw-Hill

Name _____

1. Read the following sentences from a journal entry:

   Lucy tried to make the bus. Her body lurched towards the closing door.
   John made it on the bus, but later on he missed his stop. When he realized
   the mistake, he slammed his fist against his knee and sighed loudly.

2. Pick one moment from the journal entry.

3. Write 3 more showing sentences about what happened in that moment to
   make it more focused. The sentences can be about what happened next, or
   can be more showing about what is already written.

Example: Lucy tried to make the bus. Her body lurched towards the
closing door. As it slammed shut like an alligator's mouth, Lucy's arms
fell to her sides, defeated. She stood on the corner alone and watched
the bus until it was a tiny yellow dot on the horizon. Depressed, she
adjusted her backpack, made sure her sneakers were tied, and started
on the long walk to school.

_____

_____

_____

_____

_____

_____

More Practice: Pick a different moment from the journal entry and write
3 more showing sentences about that moment.

_____

_____

_____

_____

_____

_____

© Macmillan/McGraw-Hill

 W 1.0 Writing Strategies

Name _____

A common way to spell a **long vowel** sound is to use the pattern vowel-consonant-silent **e**. Some examples: *gate*, *hide*, *eve*, *lone*, *mute*. There are also other ways to form long vowel sounds. The letter **y** can stand for the long *i* sound, as in *fly*. Two vowels together are called a diphthong and can stand for one sound. For example, the **ea** in *mean* stands for the long e sound. Other diphthongs that stand for long vowel sounds include **ee, ai,** and **oa.**

Look at each item. Fill in the missing vowel(s) to spell the sound. Then write the complete word in the space.

Vowels and Diphthongs

a	e	i	o	u	y	ee	ea	ai	oa

1. st____m   long *e*   _____

2. f____n____   long *i*   _____

3. f____nt   long *a*   _____

4. h____g____   long *u*   _____

5. c____cle   long *i*   _____

6. l____n   long *o*   _____

7. n____l   long *a*   _____

8. r____d   long *e*   _____

9. enc____clopedia   long *i*   _____

10. d____m____   long *o*   _____

© Macmillan/McGraw-Hill

Name _____

reputation	uttered	migrant	illegally
ruptured	mistreated	wrath	quickened

A. Write the vocabulary word that matches each clue.

1. If something is spoken, it is this. _____

2. If you treated someone badly, you have done this to them.

   _____

3. This is a synonym for *anger*. _____

4. This is an antonym for *slowed*. _____

5. This means the same thing as *burst*. _____

6. If something is done unlawfully, it is done this way. _____

7. A person who moves from place to place is called this.

   _____

8. Your actions affect this, the way people see you. _____

B. Write sentences using four of the vocabulary words from above.

9. _____

   _____

10. _____

    _____

11. _____

    _____

12. _____

    _____

© Macmillan/McGraw-Hill

A. Read each scenario. Then identify the author's purpose for writing it: *to inform, to entertain,* **or** *to persuade.*

1. An author writes a personal memoir about an experience with a mentor.

   Author's Purpose: _____

2. A journalist writes about a mentoring program at the local high school.

   Author's Purpose: _____

3. An author writes a short story about a boy and his mentor.

   Author's Purpose: _____

4. The mayor gives a speech asking people to join a new mentoring program.

   Author's Purpose: _____

5. A person writes a guidebook to train youth mentors.

   Author's Purpose: _____

B. Use the lines below to recommend an author whose work you really like to a friend. In your recommendation, tell your friend what you like best about the author's writing, and explain what you think the author's purpose is for writing a specific piece.

_____

_____

_____

_____

_____

_____

_____

_____

_____

_____

Name _____

As you read *Breaking Through*, fill in the Author's Purpose Chart.

Clues	Author's Purpose

How does the information you wrote in this Author's Purpose Chart help
you monitor your comprehension of *Breaking Through*?

R 2.0 Reading Comprehension (Focus on Informational Materials)

Name _____

As I read, I will pay attention to pauses, stops, and intonation.

	Mica's first day in the new house was terrible. She hated
11	it. She wanted to go back and be with Mariana. The only
23	good thing about the new house was that she didn't have to
35	share a room with Maggie anymore. Maggie was only
44	six years old, but she thought she was Mica's age. She would
56	do everything Mica did. She would borrow Mica's clothes
65	and belongings without permission. But not anymore: Mica
73	could just lock Maggie out anytime she wanted.
81	During that first week, neighbor after neighbor came over
90	to welcome the Flores family to the neighborhood. There
99	were lots of neighbors, but Mica didn't see anyone her age.
110	This made her even more depressed. She began to wonder
120	what her new school would be like. She would find out the
132	next day.
134	Mica didn't want to get up the next morning. She was
145	excited about her first day of middle school, but she didn't
156	know what to expect. Then Mica slowly rolled out of bed
167	after her mother had yelled for the fifth time for her to get up.
181	Mica locked her door and started to get ready. 190

Comprehension Check

1. How does the author make the reader feel sympathy for Mica? **Author's Perspective** The autho makes the reader feel Sympathy for Mica because she worries that she won't have any friend

2. What do you think will happen to Mica when she goes to school? **Make Predictions**

	Words Read	–	Number of Errors	=	Words Correct Score
First Read		–		=	
Second Read		–		=	

 R 1.1 Read aloud narrative and expository text fluently and accurately and with appropriate pacing, intonation, and expression.

A **schedule** lists times, places, or events in a table. The schedule below shows the day, times, and destinations for a cruise ship, the *Norwegian Sky,* from New England to Canada.

Schedule for the *Norwegian Sky*

Day	Port of Call	Arrival	Departure
1	Boston, Massachusetts	-----	6:00 P.M.
2	Sydney, Nova Scotia	8:00 A.M.	2:00 P.M.
3	Corner Brook, Newfoundland	8:00 A.M.	5:00 P.M.
4	Quebec City, Quebec	8:00 A.M.	-----
5	Quebec City, Quebec	-----	12:30 A.M.
6	Halifax, Nova Scotia	8:00 A.M.	8:00 P.M.
7	Bar Harbor, Maine	6:00 A.M.	5:00 P.M.
8	Boston, Massachusetts	9:00 P.M.	-----

Use the schedule to answer the questions.

1. How many days does the schedule show? _____

2. On what day and at what time does the ship arrive in Halifax, Nova Scotia?

_____

3. On what day and at what time does the ship depart Quebec City?

_____

4. Where will the ship be on Day 7? _____

5. In which place will the ship stay the longest?

_____

6. In which city (other than Boston) is the stay the shortest?

_____

CA **R 2.1** Identify the structural features of popular media (e.g., newspapers, magazines, online information) and use the features to obtain information.

Name _____

Meanings of words are often based on roots and base words. Words that are related are called **word families**. You can build a word family by thinking of all the parts of speech a word can be.

Word family for *illegally*: legally, legal, legality, illegal, legalize, legalization

A. Build a word family for each of the words listed. List as many related words as possible. List at least three for each word. Use a dictionary if necessary.

1. migrant: move better, lives, condition.
   _____

2. mistreated: unfaly, bad, wrong
   _____

3. quickened: needed, help, fast, helpful,
   _____

4. mentor: trusted, experienced
5. uttered: _____

B. Write sentences using five of the word family words that you listed above.

6. She is a migrant tha came here for new life

7. She mentroly train
   _____

8. _____

9. _____

10. _____

Name _____

Using the Word Study Steps

1. LOOK at the word.

2. SAY the word aloud.

3. STUDY the letters in the word.

4. WRITE the word.

5. CHECK the word.
   Did you spell the word right?
   If not, go back to step 1.

A. Find the Words

**Find and circle the spelling words in the puzzle below.
The words will be found from left to right, or top to bottom.**

```
a s l o p e a c b f t o t e b l e a k m e f o f
t h r l e k c u a u s u t e l o t c u e t o t o
h r h y m e o p t s h r i n e h w u r e p a v e
r l a b l e a c h e u s l o a n l t s k t l u n
e n a c d n x r e m o t e z g a z e r l s m a o
```

B. Make a Puzzle

**Make up a puzzle of your own using the space on this page. Give
it to someone else to solve. Be sure to use at least five spelling
words in your puzzle.**

© Macmillan/McGraw-Hill

CA **LC 1.5** Spell frequently misspelled words correctly
(e.g., *their, they're, there*).

Name _____

A. There are five spelling mistakes in this paragraph. Circle the misspelled words. Write the words correctly on the lines below.

When Randy is left to take care of his little brother, they play at being explorers. Randy takes his horse, his brother takes his fole, and together they paive the way into a forgotten city. When they reach the tyle floor of the bathroom, the room becomes an ancient shryn. Playtime makes it much easier for Randy to coks his brother to sleep.

1. _____

2. _____

3. _____

4. _____

5. _____

B. Writing Activity

Have you ever played at being an explorer? What did you do and where did you go on your explorer's expedition? Write a letter to a friend describing such an adventure as if it were real. Use five spelling words.

_____

_____

_____

_____

_____

_____

_____

_____

_____

LC 1.5 Spell frequently misspelled words correctly
(e.g., *their, they're, there*).

- The **complete predicate** includes all of the words that tell what the subject does or is.
- The **simple predicate** is the main word or words in the complete predicate.
- You can sometimes correct a sentence fragment by adding a predicate.

Read each sentence. Write the complete predicate on the space provided below each example. Put parentheses around the simple predicate. (In some sentences, the complete predicate and the simple predicate may be the same.)

1. Isabel learns languages as part of her schoolwork in archaeology.

_____

_____

2. She and her classmates practice their English with each other.

_____

3. Sometimes at home Isabel speaks English or French.

_____

4. She even knows a little Chinese!

_____

5. The dean of the language department at Isabel's university approves.

_____

6. Chinese is a difficult language to learn.

_____

7. She works hard to master the characters.

_____

8. Late into the night, Isabel is often studying.

_____

© Macmillan/McGraw-Hill

Name _____

- Begin the greeting and closing of a letter with a capital letter.
- Use a comma after the greeting and closing of a friendly letter.
- Use a comma between the names of a city and a state.
- Use a comma between the day and year in a date.

Proofread the letter Ivelise wrote to her cousin Isabel. Add commas as necessary. Cross out incorrect punctuation and the letters that should be capitalized. Use correct punctuation.

1800 Fortune Avenue

Tampa FL 33624

December 11 2006

dear Isabel,

I received your letter last week, but I've been quite busy. Do you remember I told you about my history class. Well, we are learning about ancient cities like the ones you have been visiting

My homework load is heavy, but I am enjoying learning about the South American cities? Are the Maya people like the ancient Inca people I am learning about. I wish you were here so you could help me with this essay I have to write?

write soon and tell me about your trip to the Yucatan. My mom says we may be coming to Mexico City to visit soon. I can't wait to show you my photos.

your cousin

Ivelise

Name _____

A. Make a list of 5 things that happened in your day today:

1.

2.

3.

4.

5.

B. Now, pick ONLY ONE, and write 5 sentences about that moment ONLY.

Example: Ran a mile.

I whizzed around the track like a racecar, but that was only my first lap. I slowed down and tried to pace myself, trying to breathe in through my nose and out through my mouth. My feet pounded the pavement—slap, slap, slap, slap. As I rounded the 3rd bend, I could hear my heart pounding. "Only two more laps," I reassured myself.

_____

_____

_____

_____

_____

More Practice: Try the same exercise focusing on a different moment from your day.

_____

_____

_____

_____

© Macmillan/McGraw-Hill

Name _____

Some words don't follow regular spelling patterns. Pay attention to these words when you are reading and writing. Think about how the word looks and think of other words that have the same pattern.

could   **sh**ould   **w**ould

A. Circle the word that best answers the question and write it on the line.

1. Which word means "they are"? _____

   their   they're

2. Which word rhymes with *dough*? _____

   though   tough

3. Which word rhymes with *steak*? _____

   teak   break

4. Which word has a silent letter? _____

   faster   listen

5. Which word has two sets of double letters? _____

   embarrass   choose

6. Which word rhymes with *tend*? _____

   fiend   friend

B. Circle the word that best completes each sentence.

7. How did reading the book (affect, effect) you?

8. The pens and pencils are over (there, their).

9. Moving to a new country had a big (affect, effect) on my life.

10. (Their, They're) reading and writing poetry.

© Macmillan/McGraw-Hill

 R 1.0 Word Analysis, Fluency, and Systematic Vocabulary Development

Name _____

| isolated | connection | immigrants | poverty | probably |

A. Choose the word from the box that best replaces the underlined word or words. Write it on the line.

1. You may feel a <u>link</u> to the author of your favorite book. _____

2. If you enjoy one book by an author, you will <u>most likely</u> enjoy his or her other books. _____

3. Don't make visiting your library a <u>one-time only</u> event. _____

4. Many people have escaped <u>the condition of not having enough money</u> through reading and teaching themselves. _____

5. Some <u>people who have moved from one country to another</u> use books to learn about their new culture. _____

B. Choose three vocabulary words and write a sentence for each.

6. _____
   _____

7. _____
   _____

8. _____
   _____

 R 1.0 Word Analysis, Fluency, and Systematic Vocabulary Development

Name _____

Being able to identify the **main idea** of an article and the **details** that support it will help you better understand what you read.

Read the passage. Then list the main idea and three supporting details.

One of the most difficult parts about writing is getting started. One way to make sure you have plenty of ideas to write about is to keep a writing journal. A writing journal is a place to record your thoughts, feelings, and ideas. Try keeping your journal in your backpack so you have it with you when something inspires you. Don't worry about making your journal entries perfect. Focus on recording your feelings and ideas so that you can refer to them later. If you make a habit of writing in your journal on a regular basis, you will have plenty of ideas to choose from for your next writing assignment.

Main Idea: _____

_____

Supporting Details: _____

_____

_____

_____

_____

_____

R 2.3 Connect and clarify main ideas by identifying their relationships to other sources and related topics.

© Macmillan/McGraw-Hill

As you read *A Life in Words*, fill in the Main Idea and Details Chart.

Main Idea _____

_____

Detail 1 _____

_____

Detail 2 _____

_____

Summary _____

_____

_____

How does the information you wrote in your Main Idea and Details Chart help you summarize *A Life in Words*?

R 2.4 Clarify an understanding of texts by creating outlines, logical notes, summaries, or reports.

© Macmillan/McGraw-Hill

Name _____

As I read, I will pay attention to expression.

	Have you ever asked yourself how birds and insects fly?
10	Or why birds can fly, but other animals can't? Human beings
21	have long studied nature and its mysteries. Over time they
31	have found some amazing ways to use what they have learned.
42	Of course, human beings can't fly. But they have reached
52	the skies by using technology to invent flying machines.
61	Some of these ideas for flying machines have come from
71	animals like birds and insects.
76	Birds are not the only animals that humans have tried to
87	copy. Today we are able to track a plane from takeoff to
99	landing thanks to a system that bats and dolphins use to
110	navigate and hunt.
113	There are other animals that are useful to people. Bees
123	help people in lots of ways, providing them with many
133	valuable products. In this book you will learn about some
143	other ways in which humans have developed technology by
152	imitating nature. 154

Comprehension Check

1. What is the main idea of this passage? **Main Idea and Details**

2. How have other animals helped people to develop flying machines? **Main Idea and Details**

	Words Read	–	Number of Errors	=	Words Correct Score
First Read		–		=	
Second Read		–		=	

R 1.1 Read aloud narrative and expository text fluently and accurately and with appropriate pacing, intonation, and **expression**.

© Macmillan/McGraw-Hill

A library lists all its books, DVDs, and other materials in a card catalog. There are three cards in the card catalog for each book: an author card, a title card, and a subject card. If you know the author, the title, or the subject, you can flip through the appropriate section of the catalog.

An electronic catalog works the same way. However, you can also search by key words. For instance, you can enter an author's name and a subject, or even two or more subjects like *elephants* and *Indian*. An electronic search result will give you a numbered list of titles. Type in the number of the book and press *enter*. A screen for that particular book will come up, and give you the same information that you would find in a card catalog. It will also tell you if the book is available.

Look at the information on the following card. Then answer the questions below.

J292.13M	Press, Geraldine. *Greek Myths*. Illustrated by Eirene Zagoreas. New York, Children's Publishers, 2003. 208 p. illus. Includes famous Greek myths, retold for younger readers. 1. Literature 2. Mythology 3. Ancient Greece

1. What key words could you use to find this book? _____

_____

2. Which row would house this book?

   a. J123.93–J292.01   b. J567.93–J890.23   c. J189.32–J301.78

3. What do you need to know to find this book? _____

_____

4. What kind of work is this? _____

CA R 1.4 Use organizational features of electronic text (e.g., bulletin boards, databases, keyword searches, e-mail addresses) to locate information.

Description Writing Frame

Summarize "A Life in Words."
Use the Description Writing Frame below.

Esmeralda Santiago is a popular author of children's books. There are **many interesting facts** about her life.

One interesting fact is _____
_____
_____.

Another interesting fact is _____
_____
_____
_____.

In addition, _____
_____
_____
_____.

Children all over the world love to read Esmeralda Santiago's books.

Rewrite the completed summary on another sheet of paper. Keep it as a model for writing a summary of an article or selection using this text structure.

Name _____

You can sometimes figure out the meaning of an unfamiliar word from **context clues** in the surrounding sentences. Context clues may come before or after the new word.

Read each sentence. Use context clues to determine the meaning of the word in bold type. Write the meaning of the word. Then write a new sentence that includes the bold word.

1. Carlos is **passionate** about reading. He is so excited and enthusiastic about it that he carries a book with him everywhere he goes.

   _____

   _____

2. I like to write about my feelings. Writing in a journal is one way to express **emotions**.

   _____

   _____

3. Lida has an excellent memory. She read the poem over and over until she could **recite** it easily.

   _____

   _____

4. Mom **donated** a stack of books to our school library. She also gave some to the senior citizens' center.

   _____

   _____

© Macmillan/McGraw-Hill

R 1.4 Monitor expository text for unknown words or words with novel meanings by using word, sentence, and paragraph clues to determine meaning.

Name _____

Using the Word Study Steps

1. **LOOK** at the word.

2. **SAY** the word aloud.

3. **STUDY** the letters in the word.

4. **WRITE** the word.

5. **CHECK** the word.
   Did you spell the word right?
   If not, go back to step 1.

A. Unscramble the letters to write a spelling word.

1. fetcfe   _____

2. csacue   _____

3. hriet   _____

4. bsramears   _____

5. tdfiferne   _____

6. blbropay   _____

7. ubafletui   _____

8. ehtre   _____

9. tbhguo   _____

10. sbyu   _____

B. Write a spelling word to complete each rhyme.

11. A flimsy reason is a loose _____.

12. A fully-cooked sandwich roll is a _____ bun.

13. A collection of frightening stories is a scary _____.

14. A captured idea is a _____ thought.

15. A five-cent cucumber is a _____ pickle.

CA LC 1.5 Spell frequently misspelled words correctly
(e.g., *their, they're, there*).

Name _____

A. Circle the eight misspelled words in the passage. Write the words correctly on the lines below.

If you are like many writers, you've probibly felt the efect of writer's block. A minit turns into an hour, and your paper is still blank. The next time you are cought in this trap, try writing about whatever comes to mind. Did your little sister do something to embarass you? Did you see a beutiful flower on the way to school? Your life is probably full of things to write about. Many writers create there best work by writing about what they know.

1. _____   4. _____   7. _____

2. _____   5. _____   8. _____

3. _____   6. _____

B. Writing Activity

Write a review of a book by your favorite author. Tell why you like this book so much. Use at least four spelling words.

_____
_____
_____
_____
_____
_____
_____
_____

LC 1.5 Spell frequently misspelled words correctly (e.g., *their, they're, there*).

Name _____

- A **compound subject** contains two or more simple subjects that have the same predicate.
- A **compound predicate** contains two or more simple predicates that have the same subject.
- You can combine two sentences by joining two subjects or two predicates with ***and, but,*** or ***or.***

Read each sentence. Write *S* if it has a compound subject and *P* if it has a compound predicate. Write each compound subject and compound predicate below. Then put parentheses around the simple subjects or predicates. (Not every sentence has a compound subject or compound predicate.)

1. My older sister, Selina, is studying hard and hopes to be an inventor one day. NO

   My older sister, Selina, is studying hard. She hopes to be an inventor some day.

2. Calculus, physics, and chemistry are her favorite subjects. Not but!

   I have not did it before

3. My preferred subject has always been English literature. Yes

   _____

4. Selina rises early and arrives home late. _____

   Selina rises early, and she arrives home late.

5. Selina's teachers and classmates believe she is marked for fame and fortune. _____

   _____

6. A big title and huge corner office are of no interest to Selina. _____

   _____

LC 1.1 Use simple, **compound**, and compound-complex sentences; use effective coordination and subordination of ideas to express complete thoughts.

- Use a comma before the conjunction in a compound sentence.
- If two parts of a compound sentence are not joined by a conjunction, use a semicolon to separate the parts.

Rewrite the passage below, correcting all capitalization and punctuation mistakes. Combine any sentences you find appropriate.

everyone knows that necessity is the mother of invention the woman who invented disposable diapers was both a woman and an inventor Marion Donovan invented the disposable diaper in 1950 she used a regular cloth diaper, lined it with pieces cut from a shower curtain, and called her invention "Boaters" since no company was interested in marketing her new invention Mrs. Donovan founded her own company today disposable diapers are a big business

_____

_____

_____

_____

_____

_____

_____

© Macmillan/McGraw-Hill

CA **LC 1.1** Use simple, **compound**, and compound-complex sentences; use effective coordination and subordination of ideas to express complete thoughts.

Name _____

© Macmillan/McGraw-Hill

Writing Rubric

	4 Excellent	3 Good	2 Fair	1 Unsatisfactory
	Ideas and Content/ Genre	Ideas and Content/ Genre	Ideas and Content/ Genre	Ideas and Content/ Genre
	Organization and Focus	Organization and Focus	Organization and Focus	Organization and Focus
	Sentence Structure/ Fluency	Sentence Structure/ Fluency	Sentence Structure/ Fluency	Sentence Structure/ Fluency
	Conventions	Conventions	Conventions	Conventions
	Word Choice	Word Choice	Word Choice	Word Choice
	Voice	Voice	Voice	Voice
	Presentation	Presentation	Presentation	Presentation

Name _____

> When a vowel is followed by the letter *r* it has a different sound than a vowel that is short or long, for example, the sound *âr* in **cart**. This is called an ***r*-controlled vowel.** The *r*-controlled sound can be spelled in different ways, for example: **surf, bird,** or **work.**

Read each clue. Provide an answer that uses an *r*-controlled vowel sound. Then use each word you found in a sentence.

1. Something that is ripped is this. _____

   _____

   _____

2. This is on the side of your head. _____

   _____

   _____

3. You can play games, eat hot dogs, and see farm animals here.

   _____

   _____

   _____

4. This is something you can do in the ocean. _____

   _____

   _____

5. This is the opposite of far. _____

   _____

   _____

6. You can brush it, curl it, or put it in braids. _____

   _____

   _____

 R 1.0 Word Analysis, Fluency, and Systematic Vocabulary Development

Name _____

A. Write the vocabulary word next to its definition.

immigrated	honorable	tinkering	destination
fidget	formally	concentrate	unsteady

1. to focus or direct one's thoughts _____

2. not firm; shaky _____

3. busy in a trifling way _____

4. worthy of respect _____

5. to move in a restless way _____

6. the place to which a person is traveling _____

7. moved to live in a country where one was not born _____

8. acting with proper behavior _____

B. Choose six vocabulary words. Write sentences using these words.

9. _____
   _____

10. _____
    _____

11. _____
    _____

12. _____
    _____

13. _____
    _____

14. _____
    _____

Events in a story happen in a certain order that is called **sequence**. Understanding the sequence of events can help you better understand what you read.

Read the story. Then number the events to show the order in which they occurred.

Last night, I dreamed that I met an alien at the mall.

I went to the mall with my friend Jose, who wanted to buy a new video game. So we stopped in a video store first. Then we stopped in a shoe store that was having a sale. Jose wanted to buy a new pair of sneakers and hiking boots, but it was taking him a long time to make a decision. It was getting late, so I told him I would go buy a book and come back for him.

"Your sister said to meet her at 5:30 P.M., and it's already 5 o'clock. Let's just meet your sister in front of the ice cream store," said Jose.

"Great idea," I said. Then I headed out. I was in such a hurry that I didn't even see that I was about to run into someone until it was too late. When I told the "man" that I was sorry, he got very angry. That's when I saw the third eye on his face and the extra arms on his back. I was just about to ask what planet he was from when my alarm clock started to ring.

My alarm clock woke me up. _____

Jose and I went to the shoe store. _____

We decide to meet my sister in front of the ice cream store. _____

I left Jose to go and buy a book. _____

Jose and I went to the video store. _____

I went to sleep and began having a dream. _____

I went to the mall with my friend Jose. _____

I ran into an alien. _____

© Macmillan/McGraw-Hill

CA   R 2.0 Reading Comprehension (Focus on Informational Materials)

Name _____

As you read *LAFFF,* fill in the Sequence Chart.

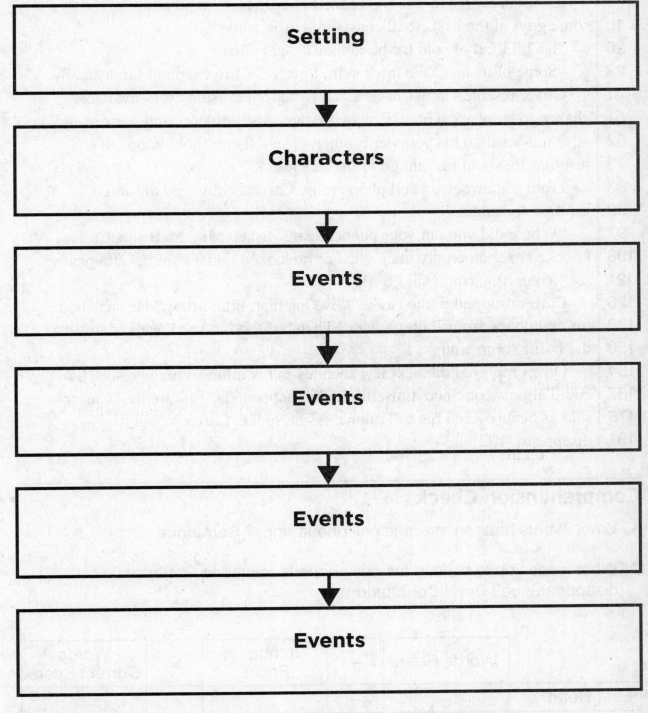

Setting

Characters

Events

Events

Events

Events

How does the information you wrote in this Sequence Chart help you monitor your comprehension of *LAFFF*?

© Macmillan/McGraw-Hill

As I read, I will pay attention to punctuation and characters' voices.

	Carter peeked over the top of the newspaper. "I'm meeting
10	some guys at the basketball courts in a little while."
20	"Isn't it kind of cold for basketball?" said Oliver.
29	"Some of us just have thick skin, I guess," Carter replied sarcastically.
41	Oliver resented how Carter acted so superior, using every available
51	chance to emphasize how he was smarter, more athletic, and more
62	adventurous than his younger brother. "Hey—I can shoot hoops. It's
73	just that Joey and I might go to the movies. . . ."
83	From somewhere, a cell phone rang. Carter rummaged around
92	for it on the table.
97	"Where did you put your phone, dear?" asked Mrs. McBride. Carter
108	knocked over an empty juice glass as he looked under napkins and plates.
121	"Ring, ring, ring," said Bailey.
126	Carter dropped to the floor. "Give me that, little missy." He snatched
138	his cell phone from Bailey's hand. Then he stood, turned, walked toward
150	the living room, and. . . .
154	Oliver replayed the next few seconds in his mind so many times, he
167	could almost convince himself it hadn't happened. "Talk to me," Carter
178	said as he answered his cell phone. As he spoke, Carter began to
191	disappear. 192

Comprehension Check

1. What events happen after the cell phone rings? **Sequence**

2. What leads you to believe the cell phone is related to Carter's disappearance? **Draw Conclusions**

	Words Read	–	Number of Errors	=	Words Correct Score
First Read		–		=	
Second Read		–		=	

 R 1.1 Read aloud narrative and expository text fluently and accurately and with appropriate pacing, intonation, and expression.

Name _____

When you need to research a topic, you can use **key words** and a search engine to explore the Internet and bring up a list of Web sites. Clicking on a Web site will bring up its home page. Usually a Web site will contain other underlined words called **hyperlinks**. Clicking on a link will take you to a Web site related to your key words.

One student found this link when he looked for information on an architect whose designs interested him.

---

http://www.franklloydwright.com/books_about.html

Frank Lloyd Wright: The Elementary School Years by Matt Plumpton

Frank Lloyd Wright's Building Blocks by Mickey Chavez

Frank Lloyd Wright's Treehouse by Wendy Willow

Toys of Frank Lloyd Wright (1893–1909) by Megan Cho

Use the information from the Web site to answer the questions.

1. What is this Web site about? _____

_____

2. What key words might the student have used to find this Web site?

_____

3. What key words would you use to find photos of the buildings Frank Lloyd Wright designed?

_____

4. How can you order a book?

_____

5. Which link would you click on to order the book by Matt Plumpton?

_____

R 2.1 Identify the structural features of popular media (e.g., newspapers, magazines, online information) and use the features to obtain information.

Synonyms are words that have the same or nearly the same meaning. Many words have the same denotation (literal meaning) but have different connotations (implied meanings, that suggest different things). For example, the words *cheap* and *inexpensive* are synonyms. *Cheap* has a negative connotation because it also includes the idea that the quality of an object is poor. The word *inexpensive* has a more positive connotation because it suggests that the object did not cost a lot of money. It has no reflection on the quality of the object.

Read each pair of synonyms. Write whether their connotations are positive or negative.

1. lean: _____

   scrawny: _____

2. old: _____

   senior: _____

3. fancy: _____

   gaudy: _____

4. ugly: _____

   plain: _____

5. careless: _____

   carefree: _____

6. thrifty: _____

   miserly: _____

7. picky: _____

   selective: _____

8. curious: _____

   nosy: _____

9. childish: _____

   playful: _____

10. stingy: _____

    frugal: _____

© Macmillan/McGraw-Hill

CA **R 1.5** Understand and explain "shades of meaning" in related words (e.g., *softly* and *quietly*).

Name _____

Using the Word Study Steps

1. LOOK at the word.
2. SAY the word aloud.
3. STUDY the letters in the word.
4. WRITE the word.
5. CHECK the word.
   Did you spell the word right?
   If not, go back to step 1.

Alphabetical Order

search	sparkle	servant	fierce	court
starve	bargain	torch	pierce	weird
rumor	parched	earnest	urge	favorite
reward	pursue	mourn	wharf	burnt

Write the spelling words in alphabetical order.

1. _____
2. _____
3. _____
4. _____
5. _____
6. _____
7. _____
8. _____
9. _____
10. _____

11. _____
12. _____
13. _____
14. _____
15. _____
16. _____
17. _____
18. _____
19. _____
20. _____

© Macmillan/McGraw-Hill

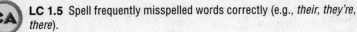 **LC 1.5** Spell frequently misspelled words correctly (e.g., *their, they're, there*).

A. There are five spelling mistakes in this story. Circle the misspelled words. Write the words correctly on the lines below.

Long ago, when James was a young boy, he worked as a mayor's servent and lived in a shed by the mayor's mansion. Late one night, the mayor's wife came to James's door with an ernest request. Her husband had gone for a walk and had not yet returned hours later. She didn't need to irge James to find her husband. James took a tortch and went to serch for him. Hours later, James found and rescued the mayor. The next day the news was all over the small town, and James became a hero. Over the years, the story of James's adventure grew until it became a grand tale.

1. _____

2. _____

3. _____

4. _____

5. _____

B. Writing Activity

How might the story of James's simple adventure have changed over the years? Write a tale that might have grown from it. Use five spelling words in your story.

_____

_____

_____

_____

_____

_____

_____

_____

_____

© Macmillan/McGraw-Hill

 LC 1.5 Spell frequently misspelled words correctly (e.g., *their, they're, there*)

Name _____

> • A **complex sentence** contains an independent clause and one or more dependent clauses.
> • When a dependent clause comes at the beginning of a sentence, use a comma after the dependent clause.
> • When a dependent clause comes at the end, a comma is not usually necessary.

Put an X in front of each complex sentence. If the dependent clause comes at the end of the sentence, rewrite the sentence so that the dependent clause comes at the beginning. If the dependent clause comes at the beginning of the sentence, rewrite it so that it comes at the end. (Note: Not every sentence is complex.)

_____ 1. While I read, I often listen to soft music.

_____

_____ 2. I have yet to find a folktale I did not enjoy.

_____

_____ 3. I usually carry a book with me wherever I go.

_____

_____ 4. I probably will not be happy until I finish reading every book on my shelf.

_____

_____ 5. My sister is always calling me a book worm.

_____

_____ 6. Before I left for school this morning, I read a tale of a brave knight.

_____

_____

_____ 7. I forgot what time it was until my mother called me.

_____

_____ 8. I find folk tales so interesting that I could read them all day.

_____

CA **LC 1.1 Use simple, compound, and compound-complex sentences;** use effective coordination and subordination of ideas to express complete thoughts.

Name _____

- A **complex sentence** contains an independent clause and one or more dependent clauses.
- When a dependent clause comes at the beginning of a sentence, use a comma after the dependent clause.
- When a dependent clause comes at the end, you usually do not use a comma.

Rewrite the passage. Draw a line under the complex sentences. Correct the capitalization and punctuation mistakes, adding punctuation as needed.

every family has its own traditions, but ours is my favorite on Sunday nights we all sit around the kitchen table with a bowl of roasted walnuts hazelnuts peanuts, and almonds as we crack the nuts each family member tells one good thing and one bad thing that happened to them that week this family time not only teaches us about each other but also lets us see that things are never all that bad

_____

_____

_____

_____

_____

_____

_____

© Macmillan/McGraw-Hill

LC 1.1 Use simple, compound, and compound-complex sentences; use effective coordination and subordination of ideas to express complete thoughts.

Name _____

Definition:

Argument: a point of view, claim, or opinion expressed in writing.

1. Read the following passage:

   Wearing uniforms makes me feel imprisoned, like I'm in someone else's fantasy of what they want me to be. It's bad enough that I can't express myself through my clothing, but now I have to wear what they want me to wear. This is unnatural, and I think that school should let me be who I really am.

2. Think about the three arguments or opinions in this passage:

   School uniforms make me feel like I'm in prison.
   I need to be able to express my personality through my clothes.
   Schools should let students be whoever they really want to be.

3. Now, choose just one of those arguments, and write two more sentences of supporting evidence. The author has given us his opinion, but hasn't really shown us why he feels so strongly. Your sentences should explain more about why the author might feel the way he does.

   _____

   _____

   _____

   _____

   _____

   _____

   _____

   _____

   _____

   _____

© Macmillan/McGraw-Hill

Compound words are words made of two or more words. Some compound words have hyphens.

fire + eater = fire-eater

When you find a compound word with a hyphen, use the single words to help you pronounce the compound word. You know that a vowel followed by an *r* has a specific *r*-controlled sound, and that the combination of vowel *ea* creates the long **e** sound.

Read each compound word below. Place a hyphen between the two words to create the correct compound words with hyphens. Then use that word in a sentence.

1. s e l f r e s p e c t _____

_____

2. o l d f a s h i o n e d _____

_____

3. w e l l b e i n g _____

_____

4. s t r o n g w i l l e d _____

_____

5. b u t t o n d o w n _____

_____

 R 1.0 Word Analysis, Fluency, and Systematic Vocabulary Development

© Macmillan/McGraw-Hill

Name _____

A. Write the vocabulary word next to its synonym.

sponsoring	array	significance	charismatic
mimics	despondently	sleuthing	anonymous

1. importance _____

2. searching _____

3. imitates _____

4. hopelessly _____

5. attractive _____

6. supporting _____

7. group _____

8. unknown _____

B. Choose four vocabulary words and write a sentence for each. Underline the vocabulary words you use in your sentences.

9. _____

_____

10. _____

_____

11. _____

_____

12. _____

_____

Name _____

Read the passage and answer the questions.

"I can't go out there," Sam said, as she peeked through the stage curtains at the ever-growing audience. "I just can't do it!" She was nearly in tears.

"Honey, you will be fantastic, really," Mrs. Mosley, Sam's drama teacher, said. "Besides, if you don't go out there, we won't have a show! You are the star, after all."

Over the last six weeks, Sam had practiced and practiced and practiced her lines. She knew them forward and backward. But they had all left her mind the minute she saw the audience—the huge crowd that would be looking right at her!

"Curtain time!" said Mrs. Mosley.

Sam, despite her knocking knees and quivering voice, walked out onstage and delivered her first line. By the time she finished her first scene, she had forgotten there even was an audience. She was a hit!

1. How does Sam feel at the beginning? _____

_____

2. What information supports this conclusion? _____

_____

3. How well is Sam prepared for the performance? Support your conclusions.

_____

_____

4. How do Sam's feelings change? Support your conclusion.

_____

_____

5. Do you think Sam will continue to act? Support your conclusion.

_____

_____

 R 2.0 Reading Comprehension (Focus on Informational Materials)

Name _____

As you read *The Case of the Phantom Poet,* fill in the
Conclusions Chart.

Text Clues	Conclusion

How does the information you wrote in this Conclusions Chart help you
monitor your comprehension of *The Case of the Phantom Poet*?

As I read, I will pay attention to dialogue, pacing, and intonation.

9	*(The stage in the school auditorium; Erica reads aloud*
19	*from a script. Joel practices karate. They are unaware that*
23	*Jesse is watching them.)*
	Erica: "Ranger: Old Teddy's going to hurt somebody soon."
32	Joel, say that line **despondently** so the audience sees how
42	upset you are. Should I write *unhappily* in the stage direction
53	instead of *despondently*?
56	**Joel:** I'm feeling despondent about this play. There's not
65	enough action in it. I should be a karate instructor instead of
77	a park ranger.
80	**Erica:** It's set in a forest. It's about a bear that gets into
93	campers' stuff. It's about how people have to learn to respect
104	animals' homes.
106	**Joel:** I could be a ranger who teaches karate in his spare time.
119	*(He chops the air and kicks one leg to the side.)* Pow! Take
132	that, Old Teddy! Erica, I'm going to make up my own lines.
144	**Erica:** You're going to ruin my play!
151	**Joel:** You're going to ruin my acting career!
159	**Erica:** A real actor follows the script and listens to what the
171	director tells him. 174

Comprehension Check

1. How would you summarize what the play is about? **Summarize**

2. How do you think this conflict between Joel and Erica will end? **Make Predictions**

	Words Read	–	Number of Errors	=	Words Correct Score
First Read		–		=	
Second Read		–		=	

 R 1.1 Read aloud narrative and expository text fluently and accurately and with appropriate pacing, **intonation**, and expression.

Name _____

Tables are used to organize information so that it is easily accessible. Columns help you organize the information into different categories. Rows help you repeat similar information.

Here is some information about some Broadway shows. *Bingo* is playing at the Starstruck. It has its first preview on December 7 and opens on January 24. *Class Zoo* is opening on March 15 at the Kids' Stage. *Class Zoo* has its first preview on February 12. *Caesar* opens at the Tall Theater in previews on March 8. *Caesar* then opens on April 3. *Western* has previews on March 26. It opens April 26 at Studio 50. The Ford Center has previews of *Iceberg* on March 29. *Iceberg* opens on April 28.

Make a table with four columns. Title your columns Play, Theater, Preview and Opening. Fill in the table with the appropriate information. Then use it to answer the questions.

1. How many shows are listed? _____

2. Which play is opening on April 3? _____

3. When is the first preview of *Class Zoo*? _____

4. Where is *Iceberg* being staged? _____

5. Which play is being performed at the Starstruck? _____

6. If you were visiting New York from March 25 to April 7, which previews could you attend? _____

Preview	Show Date	Theater	Name Play
December 7	Jan 24		
February 12			
March 29			
April 26			
March 8			

© Macmillan/McGraw-Hill

R 2.1 Identify the structural features of popular media (e.g., newspapers, magazines, online information) and use the features to obtain information.

The Case of the Phantom Poet
Grade 6/Unit 1

63

Using **analogies** requires you to understand how words relate to each other. Analogies are written like this: happy : joyful :: significance : importance. They are read like this: "Happy is to joyful as significance is to importance." **Synonyms**, words that mean the same or nearly the same thing, are often used in analogies, as in the example.

A. Choose the best word to complete the following analogies. Circle the letter of the correct answer.

1. jumped : leaped :: laughed :
   - **a.** cried
   - **b.** hoped
   - **c.** chuckled
   - **d.** smiled

2. close : shut :: perform :
   - **a.** forget
   - **b.** act
   - **c.** imitate
   - **d.** quiet

3. child : kid :: drama :
   - **a.** play
   - **b.** tragic
   - **c.** violence
   - **d.** comic

4. dinner : supper :: academy :
   - **a.** breakfast
   - **b.** title
   - **c.** obey
   - **d.** school

5. friend : pal :: author :
   - **a.** writer
   - **b.** character
   - **c.** lead
   - **d.** actor

B. Write an analogy of your own that uses synonyms.

6. _____

© Macmillan/McGraw-Hill

 R 1.0 Word Analysis, Fluency, and Systematic Vocabulary Development

Name _____

- A **run-on sentence** may be rewritten as a compound or complex sentence.

Read these sentences. If the sentence is correct, write C on the line next to it. If it is a run-on sentence, write R. Rewrite each run-on sentence.

_____ **1.** The platypus has feet like a duck's.

_____ **2.** Many scientists have studied the platypus dark brown fur covers its body.

_____

_____ **3.** Platypuses live on land, although these odd animals also swim very well.

_____

_____ **4.** The female platypus lays eggs the mother sits on the eggs like a bird.

_____

_____ **5.** The platypus has survived for millions of years many scientists call it a living fossil.

_____

_____

_____ **6.** Unlike ducks platypuses have bills that are soft and feel for food underwater.

_____

_____

Name _____

- A **sentence fragment** does not express a complete thought. You can sometimes correct a sentence fragment by adding a subject or predicate.
- A **run-on sentence** joins together two or more sentences that should be written separately.
- You can correct run-on sentences in three different ways:
  1. Separate two complete ideas in a run-on sentence into two sentences.
  2. Rewrite the run-on sentence as a compound sentence.
  3. Rewrite the run-on sentence as a complex sentence.

Correct any sentence fragments or run-on sentences in the diary entry below. Rewrite the passage with correct punctuation and capitalization.

today I joined a group of students on a bird-watching walk i wanted to see a snail kite because I read that this bird is in trouble the snail kite eats only one thing it eats the meat of the apple snail when builders drain swampland to put up buildings, the apple snails die out. then the snail kites have nothing to eat we must put a stop to putting buildings where endangered animals live

_____

_____

_____

_____

_____

_____

_____

_____

© Macmillan/McGraw-Hill

 CA LC 1.0 Written and Oral English Language Conventions

Name _____

Leash Law

by: David Milton

Dogs should have to be on a leash at the park. One day my brother was
playing basketball at the park and a dog ran up and tried to jump on him.
The owner was far away and the dog had no leash on. Leashes make dogs
uncomfortable and that's not fair to the dogs. If people are going to bring
their dogs out in public, they need to make them wear a leash so that
everybody is safe.

Definitions:

Argument: A writer's point of view
Relevant: Important or related
Irrelevant: Not important or related

1. Read the passage above.

2. Pick out the <u>irrelevant</u> sentence and underline it.

3. Now, use the sentence you chose as your main argument.

4. Write 3 more showing sentences that expand on this new argument.

_____

_____

_____

_____

_____

_____

_____

_____

_____

Plurals are often formed by adding the letter **s** to the end of a word.
   dog + s = dogs   cat + s = cats
Some words have to be changed slightly to form plurals.
   wolf   wolves   knife   knives
Sometimes, the letter **s** does not make the **/s/** sound. Instead, it makes the **/z/** sound.

A. Write the words that have an *s* that makes a /z/ sound.

1. Team spirit is not just for baseball teams. _____

2. You and your classmates can work together to meet goals.

   _____

3. Team spirit is about working together as equals. _____

4. You can work together to solve problems. _____

5. Members of a team do their best to make their plans successful.

   _____

6. Teams can succeed if they use the strengths of each member.

   _____

B. Write some sentences of your own that contain plurals that have the /z/ sound.

7. _____

   _____

8. _____

   _____

9. _____

   _____

10. _____

    _____

© Macmillan/McGraw-Hill

 R 1.0 Word Analysis, Fluency, and Systematic Vocabulary Development

Name _____

Complete the crossword using the vocabulary words.

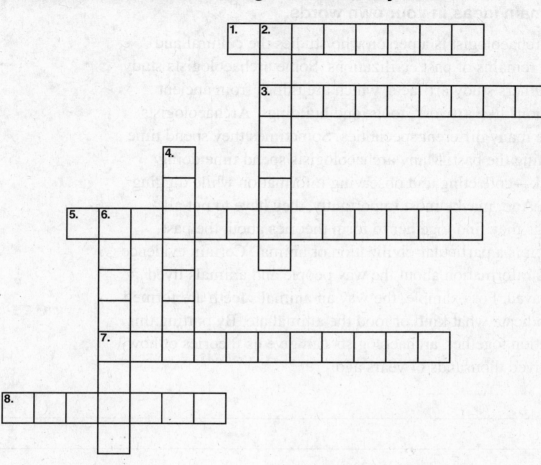

Across

1. put back into an original state

3. culturally developed

5. having a belief in chance

7. firmly

8. to lengthen in time

Down

2. to dig up

4. to come before

6. useful tools or implements often for kitchen use

Write a summary of the paragraph on the lines provided. Be sure to state the main ideas in your own words.

An archaeologist is a person who studies the cultural and physical remains of past civilizations. Some archaeologists study bones. Others study artifacts, which are things from ancient civilizations like artwork, tools, and buildings. Archaeologists can have many different specialties. Sometimes they spend time researching the past. Many archaeologists spend time doing fieldwork—collecting and observing information while digging at a site. And, maybe most importantly, they have to put all the things they find together to form theories about the past, whether it is a particular civilization or animal. Certain evidence provides information about the way people and animals lived and behaved. For example, the way an animal's teeth are formed might indicate what kind of food the animal ate. By putting this information together, archaeologists can give us theories of how people lived thousands of years ago.

_____

_____

_____

_____

_____

_____

_____

_____

_____

_____

© Macmillan/McGraw-Hill

 R 2.4 Clarify an understanding of texts by creating outlines, logical notes, summaries, or reports.

Name _____

As you read *The Emperor's Silent Army*, fill in the Summary Chart.

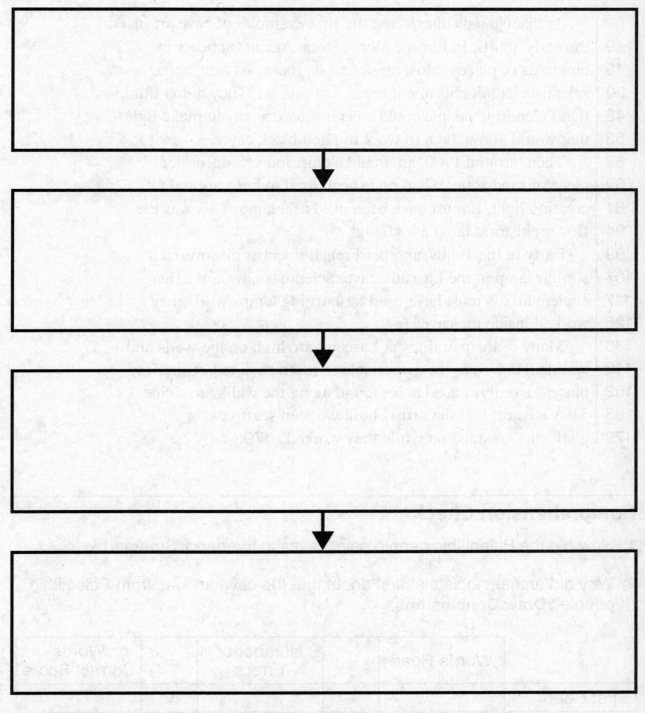

How does the information you wrote in this Summary Chart help you
monitor your comprehension of *The Emperor's Silent Army*?

Name _____

As I read, I will pay attention to the pronunciation of vocabulary and other difficult words.

9	Archaeologists discovered the first examples of cave art in the early 1800s. In Europe alone, Stone Age art appears in
19	hundreds of places. Most are found on rocks. At first, some
30	scientists had doubts about the age of this art. They didn't think
42	that Paleolithic people could have invented a way to make light
53	that would allow them to work in pitch-black caves.
62	Then, around 1900, an archaeologist found a decorated
69	piece of sandstone. It had once been used to burn animal fat,
81	creating light. It must have been used as a lamp. This was the
94	first prehistoric lamp ever found.
99	Early in the 1960s, another French scientist discovered a
107	similar lamp in the Lascaux cave. Scientists now agree that
117	ancient artists must have used fat-burning lamps while they
126	worked inside the caves.
130	Many of the paintings at Lascaux are high on the walls and
142	ceiling. How were the artists able to reach such out-of-the-way
152	places? Evenly spaced holes found along the walls are a clue.
163	They suggest that the artists built wooden scaffolds, or
172	platforms, to stand on while they worked. 179

Comprehension Check

1. How did the Paleolithic people paint caves in the dark? **Summarize**

2. Why did archaeologists at first doubt that the cave art was from Paleolithic people? **Draw Conclusions**

	Words Read	–	Number of Errors	=	Words Correct Score
First Read		–		=	
Second Read		–		=	

© Macmillan/McGraw-Hill

 CA R 1.1 Read aloud narrative and expository text fluently and accurately and with appropriate pacing, intonation, and expression.

> **Meter** is the rhythmical pattern of unstressed and stressed
> syllables in a line of poetry. Iambic pentameter, or five pairs of
> short-long syllables, is the most common meter.
>
> **Consonance** is the repetition of consonant sounds at the
> beginning or ends of two or more words grouped together. For
> example, *creak* and *crock.*

**Mark the meter of the first three lines of "Ozymandias." Underline
the stressed syllables.**

I met a traveler from an antique land

Who said: Two vast and trunkless legs of stone

Stand in the desert . . .

Circle the words that show consonance in the following lines.

Clip-clop went the horse's hooves

As she trotted across the park to be patted on the head.

Now write a short poem of your own. Use consonance in your poem.

_____

_____

_____

_____

_____

_____

_____

_____

© Macmillan/McGraw-Hill

Name _____

Words can consist of a variety of parts: prefixes, base words, suffixes, and inflectional endings. **Prefixes** are attached to the beginnings of words and often change the words' meanings.

Look at the following chart of prefixes and their meanings.

Prefix	Meaning	Example
un- **il-** **dis-**	not, without, the opposite of	unhappy illegal disappear
re-	do again	retype
super- **extra-**	beyond or above	superhuman extraordinary
anti-	against	antibiotics anti-inflammatory
bi-	two	bicycle

A. Write the meaning of each word. Use your knowledge of prefixes to help you define the words.

1. bisect: _____

2. reclassify: _____

3. unloved: _____

4. disapprove: _____

5. illiterate: _____

B. Think of three words that use the prefixes in the chart. Use a dictionary to check whether the word can take the prefix.

6. _____

7. _____

8. _____

 R 1.0 Word Analysis, Fluency, and Systematic Vocabulary Development

Name _____

Using the Word Study Steps

1. LOOK at the word.

2. SAY the word aloud.

3. STUDY the letters in the word.

4. WRITE the word.

5. CHECK the word.
   Did you spell the word right?
   If not, go back to step 1.

A. Find the Words

Find and circle the spelling words in the puzzle below.

```
A B M T O R N A D O E S R A H W O L V E S M N P
S H E L V E S D O U C S T T H I E V E S V W R O
O L D M P C S A P P H O T O S V O L C A N O E S
L A I D E U E T D D O M I N O E S O E S M R A N
O S A B U F F A L O E S A R P S H E R I F F S H
S S T A F F S O P E S O P R A N O S E N O E D R
L O A V E S C A R V E S A B N O B A C T E R I A
```

B. Make a Puzzle

Make up a puzzle of your own using the space on this page. Give it to someone else to solve. Be sure to use at least five spelling words in your puzzle.

LC 1.5 Spell frequently misspelled words correctly
(e.g., *their, they're, there*).

The Emperor's Silent Army **77**
Grade 6/Unit 2

© Macmillan/McGraw-Hill

Name _____

A. Proofreading Activity

There are five misspelled spelling words in this story. Circle the misspelled words. Write the words correctly on the lines below.

The day my friend Mickey returned from vacation, he came running over to my house to show me his fotos. He had some incredible pictures. There was one of Mickey herding a group of bufaloes. There was another of him standing on the tops of volcanos. Mickey showed me another picture of him defending himself against a pack of wolfs. The last picture was of him standing firmly on the ground while winds from gigantic tornadose destroyed everything around him.

"Why, Mickey!" I exclaimed "Seems like you had a really amazing vacation."

"No," Mickey said sheepishly. "I spent my whole vacation at my grandmother's house creating these silly pictures on her computer."

1. _____

2. _____

3. _____

4. _____

5. _____

B. Writing Activity

Have you ever imagined doing something similar to the things that Mickey does in his photos? Write about an adventure you would like to take in your life. Use five spelling words.

_____

_____

_____

_____

_____

_____

 LC 1.5 Spell frequently misspelled words correctly (e.g., *their, they're, there*).

Name _____

- Some **proper nouns** contain more than one word. Each important word begins with a capital letter.
- The name of a day, month, or holiday begins with a capital letter.

A. Identify all of the proper nouns in the following sentences. Rewrite each sentence, capitalizing all the proper nouns.

1. The broncos is a football team in our town of centerville.

_____

_____

2. mr. suarez is the coach for our rival football team, the panthers.

_____

_____

3. The broncos play on a field behind delaney creek boulevard, a main road.

_____

_____

4. Football is a popular sport in the state of florida.

_____

_____

5. The labor day kickoff party is enjoyed by all the citizens of centerville.

_____

_____

B. Write a proper noun for each of the following categories.

6. building _____

7. day of the week _____

8. month _____

9. holiday _____

10. country _____

- A **common noun** names any person, place, thing, or idea, and does not begin with a capital letter unless it begins a sentence.
- Some **proper nouns** contain more than one word. Each important word begins with a capital letter. The name of a day, month, or holiday begins with a capital letter.

Proofread this business letter for errors in capitalization and punctuation. Underline any letters you think should be capitalized. Put brackets [ ] around any letters you think should not be capitalized. Make the necessary corrections in punctuation for a business letter.

978 river road

ramsey new jersey 07446

april 15 2008

The arizona cacti

P.O. Box 1234

chandler arizona 85224

dear sir or madam

I have just begun school here in new jersey, but my Family used to live in arizona and utah. I would like to attend baseball camp during the Summer of 2008 with your organization. My Family will be traveling to arizona for the fourth of july, so the week of july 9 through july 15 would be best. Please let me know the cost of one Week of camp and any Equipment I might need to bring with me.

Thank you for your assistance.

sincerely yours

Matthew Perricone

© Macmillan/McGraw-Hill

CA LC 1.0 Written and Oral English Language Conventions

Name _____

1. Please read the following sentences and circle the verb:

   I walked home.

   I said "Cool!"

2. Rewrite each one three times, using a different and stronger verb. You can change other parts of the sentence too.

   a. _____

   b. _____

   c. _____

   a. _____

   b. _____

   c. _____

Extra Practice: Circle the verbs in these sentences and rewrite them three times with stronger verbs:

Mike threw the ball.

Zoe ate the hot fudge sundae.

When you add **-ed** or **-ing** to a word that ends with one consonant, double the consonant if the vowel that comes before it has a short sound.

trap + ed = trapped   trap + ing = trapping
shop + ed = shopped   shop + ing = shopping

Do not double the last consonant when the vowel that comes before it is long or when the word ends with more than one consonant. Just add the ending. If a word ends with a silent **e**, drop the **e** before adding the ending.

peek + ed = peeked   peek + ing = peeking
rest + ed = rested   rest + ing = resting
time + ed = timed   time + ing = timing

There are some exceptions to the rules above.

pilot + ed = piloted   pilot + ing = piloting
travel + ed = traveled   travel + ing = traveling

Read each word, and add the endings -ed and -ing to each one. Follow the rules above.

1. open _____   6. trot _____

2. close _____   7. coat _____

3. hope _____   8. cook _____

4. hop _____   9. direct _____

5. wish _____   10. deliver _____

CA R 1.0 Word Analysis, Fluency, and Systematic Vocabulary Development

A. Complete each sentence by choosing the best word from the box.

foundation	reliable	maintain	feature
promoted	restricted	regions	principal

1. In ancient Greece, kitchens were not a _____ of every home.

2. The ancient Greeks _____ sports as a way to stay fit and prepare children for the future.

3. In Athens, women were more _____ than the women in other city-states.

4. The ancient Greeks helped lay the _____ of our civilization today.

5. The people of Sparta wanted to _____ a powerful army.

6. The _____ subjects of school in ancient Greece were reading, writing, and music.

7. The _____ of Greece consisted of a city and its surrounding farmland.

8. Many families had _____ servants that they depended on.

B. Choose two vocabulary words. For each word, write a sentence of your own about your daily life.

_____

_____

_____

_____

_____

Name _____

> The **main idea** is the most important point of a text. **Supporting
> details** reinforce the main idea. When you summarize a text, you
> should include the main idea and supporting details.

**A. Read the paragraph about buildings in ancient Greece. Then
read the sentences below. If a statement is the main idea, write
M. If a statement is a detail, write *D*.**

The theater was an important part of Greek culture. The first play in
Athens took place in the fifth century B.C. It was such a success that plays
became a regular part of festivals and celebrations. Because plays were
so popular, theaters were designed to hold a large number of people. The
theater at Epidaurus seats approximately 14,000 people. People can still see
plays there today.

____ Theaters were designed to hold many people.

____ Plays became a regular part of festivals and celebrations.

____ The theater was an important part of Greek culture.

____ The first play took place in the fifth century B.C.

**B. Now summarize the paragraph. Be sure to include the main idea
and the most important details. Remember to use your own
words.**

_____

_____

_____

_____

_____

_____

_____

© Macmillan/McGraw-Hill

 R 2.3 Connect and clarify main ideas by identifying their relationships
to other sources and related topics.

Name _____

As you read *Daily Life in Ancient Greece*, fill in the Main Idea and Details Chart.

Main Idea _____

_____

Detail 1 _____

_____

Detail 2 _____

_____

Summary _____

_____

_____

_____

How does the information you wrote in this Main Idea and Details Chart help you summarize *Daily Life in Ancient Greece*?

R 2.4 Clarify an understanding of texts by creating outlines, logical notes, summaries, or reports.

As I read, I will pay attention to phrasing.

	Astronomy is the study of stars, planets, and other objects
10	in space. The term comes from two Greek words that mean
21	"star" and "to name."
25	Astronomers are people who observe stars, planets,
32	comets, and other distant objects. Modern astronomers use
40	instruments to observe the sky. They have computers to make
50	calculations about data. They record what they see on
59	computers, too. Calculators help them solve mathematical
66	problems. Powerful telescopes give them a clear look deep
75	into the universe. They launch space probes and satellites
84	into space. These broadcast photographs of planets and
92	galaxies far from Earth.
96	Ancient astronomers didn't have scientific equipment.
102	They had no binoculars or telescopes or computers. But they
112	did carefully observe the closer planets and the stars. They
122	used their eyes. What they saw helped them develop ideas
132	about the universe. They created theories about the size and
142	shape of Earth and how it was positioned in space. 152

Comprehension Check

1. What is the main idea of this passage? **Main Idea and Details**

2. How are ancient astronomers and modern astronomers alike? How are they
    different? **Compare and Contrast**

	Words Read	–	Number of Errors	=	Words Correct Score
First Read		–		=	
Second Read		–		=	

© Macmillan/McGraw-Hill

 R 1.1 Read aloud narrative and expository text fluently and accurately
and with appropriate pacing, intonation, and expression.

Name _____

Imagery is the use of words that appeal to the senses.

The brisk sea breeze made our skin *tingle*.

Similes are a kind of figurative language in which the poet compares two unlike things using the words *like* or *as*.

The boat raced *like a horse* across the sea.

A. Read the poem. Then answer the questions that follow.

The Sea

The sea is like a baby.
When it is content,
it gurgles and coos.
But when it is angry,
it shrieks and wails.

Then the storm passes.
The sea is as smooth as baby skin.
All is calm again.

1. What are two words that appeal to your sense of hearing?

_____

2. What word appeals to your sense of touch? _____

3. Write the two similes that appear in the poem. _____

_____

4. How is the sea like a baby? _____

_____

B. Now write your own simile about the sea.

_____

_____

R 3.4 Define how tone or meaning is conveyed in poetry through word choice, figurative language, sentence structure, line length, punctuation, rhythm, repetition, and rhyme.

Name _____

> **Homophones** are words that are pronounced the same but have different spellings and meanings.
>
> Example: *to, too,* and *two*
>
> If you are confused about the meaning of a homophone, you can check a dictionary.

A. Read each sentence. Underline the correct homophone to complete the sentence.

1. I plan (to, too, two) attend the Native American History Conference next week.

2. I (sea, see) that they have guest speakers from several groups.

3. I want to (hear, here) about the Trail of Tears.

4. (Their, There, They're) going to have a whole day dedicated to that historical event.

5. I hope you will (be, bee) (their, there, they're) (for, four) it.

6. I like to (pier, peer) under the (pier, peer) for clams.

B. Use another form for the homophones from the sentences above in a sentence of your own.

7. _____

_____

8. _____

_____

9. _____

_____

10. _____

_____

 R 1.0 Word Analysis, Fluency, and Systematic Vocabulary Development

Name _____

Using the Word Study Steps

1. LOOK at the word.
2. SAY the word aloud.
3. STUDY the letters in the word.
4. WRITE the word.
5. CHECK the word.
   Did you spell the word right?
   If not, go back to step 1.

A. Missing Letters

Fill in the missing letters to form spelling words.

1. reg ___ ___ ___ting
2. t ___ ___ ___ ___ ed
3. h ___ ___ ___ ___ ed
4. o ___ ___ ___ ___ ing
5. c ___ ___ ___ ___ ___ ing
6. sl ___ ___ ed
7. en ___ ___ ___ ___ aged
8. si ___ ___ ed
9. ___ ___ ___ ___ ___ eling
10. perm ___ ___ ___ ___ ___

11. l ___ ___ ___ ___ ed
12. rev ___ ___ ing
13. u ___ ___ ___ ___ ed
14. su ___ ___ ___ ___ ___ ___ ing
15. a ___ ___ ___ ed
16. r ___ ___ ___ ___ ___ ed
17. ___ ___ ___ veled
18. cr ___ ___ ___ ___ ___
19. pa ___ ___ ___ ___ ing
20. ___ ___ ___ ___ ling

B. Write the Words

Use the lines below to practice writing the spelling words.

_____ _____ _____
_____ _____ _____
_____ _____ _____
_____ _____ _____
_____ _____ _____

LC 1.5 Spell frequently misspelled words correctly (e.g., *their, they're, there*).

Daily Life in Ancient Greece
Grade 6/Unit 2   **89**

Name _____

A. Proofreading Activity

There are five spelling mistakes in this paragraph. Circle the misspelled words. Write the words correctly on the lines below.

     As I sat in the park and siped my lemonade, I marvelled at what a beautifully clear day it was. The sky was blue and flawless. Then all of a sudden, out of nowhere, a small glimmerring disc came orbitting out of the sky and hoverd above my head before plummeting to the ground. I sat there amazed for a minute, as the disc came to a halt by my feet. Had I just come into contact with something from another planet? Slightly afraid, I looked down at my feet, only to discover that what I had seen was just your average plastic flying disk.

1. _____

2. _____

3. _____

4. _____

5. _____

B. Writing Activity

Did you ever think about the possibility of life on other planets? Write a letter to an alien explaining your life on Earth. Use five spelling words.

_____

_____

_____

_____

_____

_____

_____

_____

© Macmillan/McGraw-Hill

 LC 1.5 Spell frequently misspelled words correctly (e.g., *their, they're, there*).

Name _____

> • Add **-es** to form the **plural** of singular nouns that end in **s, sh, ch,** or **x**.
> • To form the plural of nouns ending in a consonant and **y**, change the **y** to **i** and add **-es**.
> • To form the plural of nouns ending in a vowel and **y**, add **-s**.

A. Correct the misspellings of the plural nouns in these sentences.

1. Hector believes in his fantansys about becoming an astronaut.

   _____

2. He plans to begin his studys to become a pilot soon.

   _____

3. Yesterday, Hector got two boxs of books in the mail about space travel.

   _____

4. There will be no delayes for Hector in his goal to reach outer space.

   _____

5. Lots of girls and boyes at Hector's school share his dream.

   _____

B. Write the plural form of each singular noun below.

6. mix _____

7. speech _____

8. community _____

9. glass _____

10. journey _____

11. factory _____

12. flash _____

- Add **-s** to form the **plural** of most singular nouns.
- Add **-es** to form the plural of singular nouns that end in **s, sh, ch,** or **x.**
- To form the plural of nouns ending in a consonant and **y,** change the **y** to **i** and add **-es.**
- To form the plural of nouns ending in a vowel and **y,** add **-s.**

Proofread this editorial for errors in spelling and punctuation. Put brackets [ ] around any misspellings of singular or plural nouns. Add commas in a series where needed.

Editorial from the *Sun City Sentinel*:

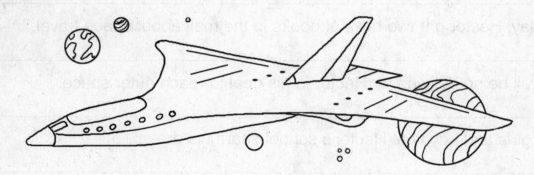

   This country spends far too much money on space travel. We have enough problem right here on Earth! We need to improve our road systems water systems and air quality. We need our communitys to band together to think of fixs for these problem. How many discoverys must astronauts make? Large quantitys of money spent on space exploration will not make Earth a better places to live! Let's get together—friendes enemys and all—no more fantasys about space!

 LC 1.0 Written and Oral English Language Conventions

Name _____

1. **Please read the following sentences, and underline the verbs:**

There is a fireplace in the room.

The room is big.

There is a tablecloth on the table.

She is smiling.

2. **Rewrite each sentence by taking out the form of verb "to be" and substituting a strong verb. You will need to add other words.**

Example: A fireplace looms over the room.

a. _____

b. _____

c. _____

d. _____

Extra Practice: Following the above instructions, rewrite these sentences:

The autumn leaves are pretty.

Dave is good at math.

Name _____

> A **closed syllable** ends in a consonant and has a short vowel sound.

**Circle the word with the closed syllable in each of the below sets.
Then write a sentence using that word.**

1. up   try   night

_____

2. go   load   lock

_____

3. sent   told   hurt

_____

4. game   why   tennis

_____

5. goat   fright   run

_____

 R 1.0 Word Analysis, Fluency, and Systematic Vocabulary Development

Name _____

A. Fill in each blank with a vocabulary word.

> anthropologists   presumably   portable   nuisance   immense

1. Communication is of _____ importance in modern daily life.

2. It is a _____ if you can't reach someone on the telephone.

3. People have been communicating _____ for thousands of years.

4. People who are _____ study the remnants of cultural communication, such as paintings and carved tablets.

5. Means of communication today, such as cell phones, are much more

   _____ than those of the past, such as stone tablets.

B. Use the vocabulary words in sentences of your own.

6. _____

   _____

7. _____

   _____

8. _____

   _____

9. _____

   _____

10. _____

    _____

Name _____

Read the passage.

Many products today are advertised in terms of **problem and solution**.
For example, hair conditioner is supposed to be a solution to the problem
of dry, tangled, and damaged hair.

**Create your own product to be used in the home. Design
an advertisement that describes a problem and tells how your
product will provide the solution to that problem. Draw your
advertisement in the box. Then use your advertisement to
answer the questions below.**

```
┌─────────────────────────────────────────────────────┐
│                                                       │
│                                                       │
│                                                       │
│                                                       │
│                                                       │
│                                                       │
│                                                       │
│                                                       │
│                                                       │
│                                                       │
└─────────────────────────────────────────────────────┘
```

1. What is the name of your product? _____

2. What problem does your product solve?

   _____

   _____

3. How does your product solve the problem?

   _____

   _____

   _____

   _____

 R 2.0 Reading Comprehension (Focus on Informational Materials)

As you read *These Walls Can Talk*, fill in the Problem and Solution Chart.

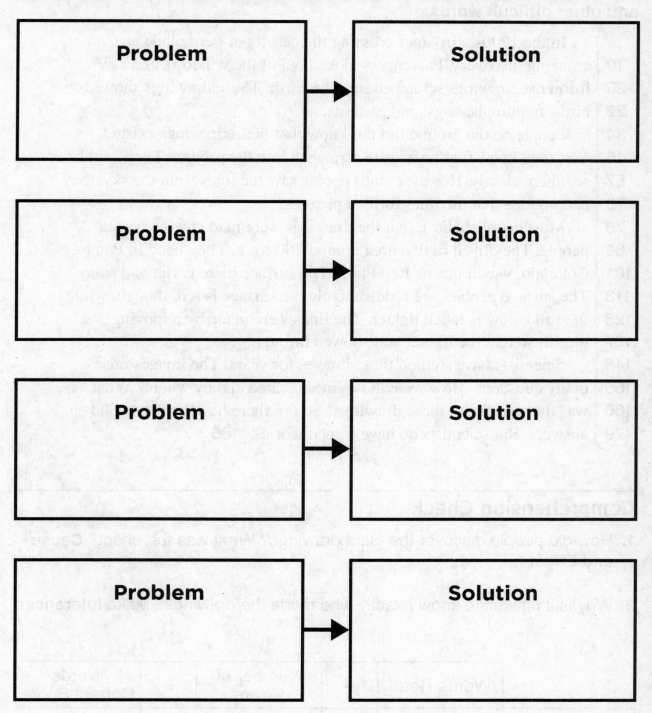

Problem	Solution
Problem	Solution
Problem	Solution
Problem	Solution

How does the information you wrote in this Problem and Solution Chart
help you monitor your comprehension of *These Walls Can Talk*?

© Macmillan/McGraw-Hill

As I read, I will pay attention to the pronunciation of vocabulary and other difficult words.

	In the 1900s, airplanes crossing the deserts of Peru made an
10	amazing discovery. Passengers looked out of the windows and saw
20	**immense** drawings scratched into the earth. These drawings showed
29	birds, mammals, bugs, and patterns.
34	People on the ground did not know that these drawings existed.
45	Yes, they knew that lines were scratched into the ground. They could
57	see them clearly. However, until people saw the lines from the sky, they
70	had no idea that the lines formed pictures.
78	Most people believe that the drawings were made by the Nazca
89	people. They lived in that area around 200 B.C.E. They lived in Pampa
101	Colorado, which means Red Plain. The surface there is flat and stony.
113	The surface pebbles are reddish. Only the surface is red, though, while
125	the soil below is much lighter. The lines were made by removing
137	topsoil so that the lighter soil showed through.
145	Scientists have studied these images for years. The images raise
155	many questions. How were these lines created and by whom? What
166	was the purpose of these drawings? So far, there have been no solid
179	answers. But scientists do have some theories. 186

Comprehension Check

1. How did people discover the giant drawings? What was the effect? **Cause and Effect**

2. Why is it difficult to know exactly who made the drawings? **Make Inferences**

	Words Read	−	Number of Errors	=	Words Correct Score
First Read		−		=	
Second Read		−		=	

© Macmillan/McGraw-Hill

 R 1.1 Read aloud narrative and expository text fluently and accurately and with appropriate pacing, intonation, and expression.

Functional documents give you information to help you complete tasks, decide on purchases, or get from one place to another. They might also provide information about an organization or community. It is important to be able to interpret such documents in order to access the information you need.

What if you were going to see a friend at his house? You have never been there before. He gives you these directions. Read the directions and then answer the questions.

1. Walk down Duffield Street until you run into Tillary Street.
2. Turn right on Tillary Street.
3. Make an immediate left on Flatbush Avenue.
4. Walk down Flatbush Avenue, past the gas station.
5. Turn right on Myrtle Avenue. There is a restaurant on the corner.
6. Walk down Myrtle Avenue. At the second stoplight, turn right onto Ashland Place.
7. My house is on the right, before you get to Willoughby Street.

1. What is the purpose of this functional document? _____
_____

2. What is the first turn that you would make? _____
_____

3. How many streets will you walk on to get to your friend's house? _____

4. Where is your friend's house located? _____
_____

5. What markers does your friend use to help you find the streets? _____
_____

© Macmillan/McGraw-Hill

Name _____

Problem/Solution Writing Frame

A. Summarize *These Walls Can Talk*.
Use the Problem/Solution Writing Frame below.

Ancient cave drawings are deteriorating at a rapid rate.

This is a **problem** because

_____
_____
_____
_____
_____ .

To **solve** this problem, _____

_____
_____
_____
_____ .

Other people have, _____

_____
_____
_____
_____
_____ .

B. Many efforts are being made to preserve these ancient masterpieces.

Rewrite the completed summary on another sheet of paper. Keep it as a model for writing a summary of an article or selection using this text structure.

 R 2.0 Reading Comprehension

Name _____

Words can be made up of prefixes, suffixes, and roots. Roots are different from word bases because they cannot stand alone. Many words in the English language trace their history back to Greek and Latin. If you learn the meanings of several basic Greek and Latin **word parts**, you will unlock the key to a larger English vocabulary. Knowing the basic meanings will allow you to grasp the meanings of seemingly unfamiliar words.

Review the chart. Use the meanings of the word parts to help you define the words below.

Root	Meaning	Example
ject	throw	*eject*
auto	self	*automobile*
bio	life	*biology*
graph	write	*autograph*
tele	far away	*telescope*
manu	hand	*manufacture*
cent	one hundred	*centuries*
logy	science of	*zoology*

1. reject: _____

2. autograph: _____

3. manuscript: _____

4. centennial: _____

5. zoology: _____

6. telephone: _____

7. manual: _____

8. biology: _____

R 1.3 Recognize the origins and meanings of frequently used foreign words in English and use these words accurately in speaking and writing.

Using the Word Study Steps

1. LOOK at the word.

2. SAY the word aloud.

3. STUDY the letters in the word.

4. WRITE the word.

5. CHECK the word.
Did you spell the word right?
If not, go back to step 1.

A. Find Rhyming Words

Circle the word in each row that rhymes with the spelling word on the left.

1. **mental**	lintel	gentle	mindless
2. **dwelling**	rebel	climbing	swelling
3. **snapshot**	plot	blank	cap
4. **ponder**	winner	wander	wonder
5. **pumpkin**	bumpkin	stumped	flint
6. **funnel**	run	tunnel	camel
7. **factor**	tractor	lecture	alligator
8. **banner**	runner	junior	manor
9. **necklace**	glass	reckless	trace
10. **ballot**	bullet	slot	palette

B. Write a poem of at least four lines. Include two of the spelling words in your poem.

_____

_____

_____

_____

© Macmillan/McGraw-Hill

 LC 1.5 Spell frequently misspelled words correctly (e.g., *their, they're, there*).

A. Proofreading Activity

There are five misspelled spelling words in this story. Circle the misspelled words. Write the words correctly on the lines below.

Last year, I started a small detective business in my town. When a crime occurs, people come to me to solve it. Today, around 4:30 p.m., my friend Jahlani Philips came to me. He said that his mother was on her way to her friend's house last night when she noticed that the neckless she intended to wear was missing.

I immediately followed him to his house to interview the viktim. Once there, I asked her if she had any pictures of the stolen goods. She handed us a snapposht of the diamond jewelry. I then asked Jahlani's mother to recall her activities from yesterday. She explained that she had been wearing the jewelry all day, but took it off in the afternoon while she was making a pumcken pie. When she went to put it back on, she realized it was gone.

"Where did you take off your jewelry?" I asked.

"Why, in my bedroom, of course, and I placed it back into my jewelry box just like I always do. When I returned to get it for the party, it was gone."

"Do you mind if I have a look around?" I asked, heading for the kitchen.

"Not at all," she replied.

Upon opening the door to the pantree, I uncovered the missing necklace. Jahlani's mother was so happy with my discovery, she gave me a hug.

1. _____   2. _____   3. _____

4. _____   5. _____

B. Writing Activity

Have you ever lost something important to you? Write about a time when you thought you had lost an important object and how you felt when you found it. Use five spelling words.

_____

_____

_____

_____

CA **LC 1.5** Spell frequently misspelled words correctly
(e.g., *their, they're, there*).

These Walls Can Talk   103
Grade 6/Unit 2

Name _____

- To form the plural of nouns that end with a vowel and **o**, add **-s**.
- To form the plural of nouns that end with a consonant and **o**, add **-s** or **-es**.
- Some nouns have special plural forms.
- A few nouns have the same singular and plural forms.

Write the plural form of each singular noun below.

1. mouse _____

2. rodeo _____

3. potato _____

4. ox _____

5. concerto _____

6. silo _____

7. wolf _____

8. self _____

9. child _____

10. moose _____

11. headquarters _____

12. knife _____

13. ratio _____

14. mix _____

15. goose _____

CA LC 1.0 Written and Oral English Language Conventions

Name _____

- To form the plural of most nouns ending in *f* or *fe*, add *-s*.
- For other nouns, change the *f* to *v* and add *-es*.
- To form the plural of nouns that end with a vowel and *o*, add *-s*.
- To form the plural of nouns that end with a consonant and *o*, add *-s* or *-es*.
- Some nouns have special plural forms that must be memorized.
- A few nouns have the same singular and plural forms.

Proofread this passage. Then rewrite the passage using the correct plural form. Correct any mistakes in capitalization or punctuation.

since I live in florida, I have a lot of personal experience with hurricanes. This summer, four hurricanes hit the state of florida my parents made sure we had plenty of canned food water and diapers for the baby batterys were in short supply at the store, and all the familys on my street rushed out to buy the few battery-powered radioes left on the store shelfs we were safe and dry in our house we had three loafs of bread and lots of peanut butter

_____

_____

_____

_____

_____

_____

_____

_____

Writing Rubric

4 Excellent	3 Good	2 Fair	1 Unsatisfactory
Ideas and Content/ Genre	Ideas and Content/ Genre	Ideas and Content/ Genre	Ideas and Content/ Genre
Organization and Focus	Organization and Focus	Organization and Focus	Organization and Focus
Sentence Structure/ Fluency	Sentence Structure/ Fluency	Sentence Structure/ Fluency	Sentence Structure/ Fluency
Conventions	Conventions	Conventions	Conventions
Word Choice	Word Choice	Word Choice	Word Choice
Voice	Voice	Voice	Voice
Presentation	Presentation	Presentation	Presentation

CA W 1.0 Writing Strategies

Name _____

An **open syllable** ends in a vowel. The vowel sound is long.

music   **fe**male   **pre**fix

A. Circle the word with the open syllable. Write it on the line.

1. The Incas were a _____ culture.

   tribal   splendid   warring

2. They had a strict _____ structure.

   business   military   social

3. They grew_____.

   corn   beans   potatoes

4. They used llamas for _____.

   farming   labor   companions

5. They built forts from _____ stones.

   giant   massive   rough

**B. Circle the word in each pair that has an open syllable. Then write a
word that rhymes with the word you circled.**

6. local   locket   _____

7. tidbit   tidal   _____

8. crazy   cranberry   _____

9. reckon   recent   _____

10. regal   regular   _____

Name _____

Use the clues to complete the crossword.

remote   withstood   venomous   vegetation
accompanied   interpreter   escort   foretold

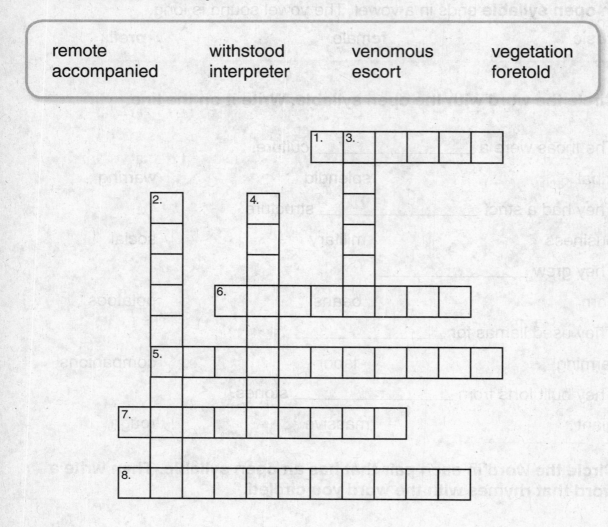

Across

1. secluded
5. went with as a companion
6. predicted
7. resisted the effect of
8. person who translates

Down

2. plants
3. a person who accompanies another to give protection
4. poisonous

 R 1.0 Word Analysis, Fluency, and Systematic Vocabulary Development

Read the passage. Then answer the questions.

"How does a whole city get lost?" Todd asked his mother.

"It isn't actually lost," she explained. "It's more like people forgot it was there."

Todd was very excited. He and his mother were on their way to visit Machu Picchu. It was the first time Todd and his mother would be going to Peru.

The tour guide explained that Machu Picchu, or at least what was left of it, was discovered by a man named Hiram Bingham. Todd listened intently as the tour guide described the dangers Bingham and his crew faced while trying to reach the city—a city they were not sure even existed!

"At least we don't have to cut our way through the forest to get there," Todd said. His mother agreed.

When the tour guide finished, both Todd and his mother settled into their train seats to take in the view of the rain forest.

Todd tried to imagine the way Bingham had felt as he climbed the mountain. Todd could hardly wait to see the actual city. It was going to be one of the best times of his life, he was sure. When he finally arrived, he was not disappointed.

1. What happens in the story? _____

_____

2. Who is the main character of the story? _____

3. Where is the story set? _____

_____

4. How does Todd feel about seeing Machu Picchu? _____

_____

5. What does Todd learn on the way? _____

_____

Name _____

Ta-Na-E-Ka

As you read *Lost City*, fill in the Character, Setting, Plot Chart.

Character	Setting	Plot
Mrs Richards on Roger Dearleg Amos Deerleg Mary	woods rivers	Mary doen't want to complete hair Ta-Na-E-ka (10 daus) -Survival test
Mary's Mom Flat Nose (know chief)		-no tools -started Ta-Na-E ka -Mary nas $5
		-she lived arestaurant for 5 daus

How does the information you wrote in this Character, Setting, Plot
Chart help you analyze the story structure of *Lost City*?

 R 2.0 Reading Comprehension (Focus on Informational Materials)

© Macmillan/McGraw-Hill

Name _____

As I read, I will pay attention to phrasing and intonation.

	Abdullah (Ahb-DUL-lah) loosened his black-and-white
4	head covering. Another grueling day of work was under way.
14	His job was to help remove dirt from ancient tombs, or
25	graves. Abdullah looked around the excavation site and tried
34	to count all of the exposed graves. But he soon gave up.
46	"There are too many of them," he thought. "Besides, if
56	Sheik Hamoudi (shayk hah-MOOD-ee) catches me counting
61	graves instead of working, he will send me away." Abdullah
71	threw himself into removing dirt, but while he worked,
80	he secretly dreamed of discovering a hidden treasure.
88	Sheik Hamoudi was the foreman on the site. He had
98	worked for the Englishman for a long time. For the past
109	week, the Sheik had been the boss while the Englishman and
120	his wife were away in Baghdad. He treated his workers fairly,
131	and yet he frightened Abdullah when he yelled. Abdullah had
141	grown up in the south of Iraq and had never been more than
154	a few miles from his village. 160

Comprehension Check

1. What words would you use to describe Abdullah? **Character, Setting, Plot**

2. What does Abdullah dream of finding? **Character, Setting, Plot**

	Words Read	–	Number of Errors	=	Words Correct Score
First Read		–		=	
Second Read		–		=	

© Macmillan/McGraw-Hill

R 1.1 Read aloud narrative and expository text fluently and accurately and with appropriate pacing, **intonation**, and expression.

Social studies includes information about government, economics, geography, and history. Here are some special features that might help you use a social studies **textbook**.

a. **Table of contents**—lists the book's units and chapters and their page numbers

b. **Headings and subheadings**—identifies the contents of the page, section, or paragraph

c. **Glossary**—defines specific terms used in the text

d. **Index**—alphabetically lists subjects in the book with their page numbers

e. **Captions for photographs**—often provide information about the subject

Answer the questions by writing the letter of the correct feature.

1. Where would you look for the beginning page number for Chapter 3? ____

2. Where would you look if you wanted to find information on Julius Caesar? ____

3. Where would you look to find out what the word *triumvirate* means? ____

4. Where would you look to find out what the article on page 156 concerns? ____

5. Where would you look to locate information on ancient Rome? ____

6. Where would you find information about a photograph of the Grand Canyon? ____

7. Where could you look to find the date of the beginning of World War I? ____

8. Where would you find the definition of *treaty*? ____

9. Where would you find further information about a specific topic? ____

10. Where would you find the page number of the beginning of a chapter on Japan? ____

© Macmillan/McGraw-Hill

R 2.1 Identify the structural features of popular media (e.g., newspapers, magazines, online information) and use the features to obtain information.

Compound words are words that consist of two or more words joined together. They can be hyphenated, closed, or open. If you are not sure how to write a compound word, look it up in the dictionary.

sister-in-law   everybody   roller skate

You can use the separate parts of compound words to determine their meaning.

under + growth = undergrowth

Low plants on the floor of a forest.

A. Identify the separate words that make up each compound word. Explain how they create the meaning of the word.

1. foretold _____

_____

_____

2. snowcapped _____

_____

_____

3. stonework _____

_____

_____

4. staircase _____

_____

_____

B. Write a sentence using a compound word. You may use one listed above, or you may choose one on your own.

5. _____

_____

Name _____

Using the Word Study Steps

1. LOOK at the word.
2. SAY the word aloud.
3. STUDY the letters in the word.
4. WRITE the word.
5. CHECK the word.
   Did you spell the word right?
   If not, go back to step 1.

A. Write the spelling words in alphabetical order.

1. _____   11. _____
2. _____   12. _____
3. _____   13. _____
4. _____   14. _____
5. _____   15. _____
6. _____   16. _____
7. _____   17. _____
8. _____   18. _____
9. _____   19. _____
10. _____   20. _____

B. Write the Words

Use the lines below to practice writing the spelling words.

_____ _____ _____ _____

_____ _____ _____ _____

_____ _____ _____ _____

_____ _____ _____ _____

_____ _____ _____ _____

 LC 1.5 Spell frequently misspelled words correctly
(e.g., *their, they're, there*).

Name _____

A. Proofreading Activity

Circle the five misspelled words in the passage. Write the words correctly on the lines below.

Last year, before my brother went off to college, my family took a vacation to Maine for a week. We stayed in cabends umid the trees and tried to forus on just spending time together. Though I still see my brother all the time, I can't ressist thinking that our vacation last summer will remain a vitale memory for me.

1. _____   2. _____   3. _____
4. _____   5. _____

B. Writing Activity

Have you ever had to say good-bye to a good friend or family member when they moved away? Write a description of what it was like for them to leave. Use at least five spelling words.

_____
_____
_____
_____
_____
_____
_____
_____
_____
_____
_____

CA **LC 1.5** Spell frequently misspelled words correctly (e.g., *their, they're, there*).

Lost City • Grade 6/Unit 2   115

- A plural **possessive noun** is a plural noun that shows ownership.
- To form the possessive of a plural noun that ends in **-s**, add an apostrophe.
- To form the possessive of a plural noun that does not end in **-s**, add an apostrophe and **-s**.

Write the plural possessive for each of the singular possessive nouns below.

1. writer's _____
2. boss's _____
3. story's _____
4. farmer's _____
5. man's _____
6. husband's _____
7. villager's _____
8. daughter's _____
9. father's _____
10. mother's _____
11. buffalo's _____
12. child's _____
13. thief's _____
14. woman's _____
15. moose's _____
16. mouse's _____
17. wolf's _____
18. zoo's _____
19. ox's _____
20. century's _____

© Macmillan/McGraw-Hill

CA **LC 1.0** Written and Oral English Language Conventions

Name _____

- Add **-s** to most nouns to form the plural. Do not use an apostrophe.
- Add an apostrophe and **-s** to a singular noun to make it **possessive**.
- Add an apostrophe to make most plural nouns possessive. Add **'s** to plural nouns that do not end in **-s**.

Proofread this persuasive essay. Then rewrite the essay using the correct possessive or plural form of the nouns. Add apostrophes and -s where needed to form possessive nouns. Correct any mistakes in capitalization or punctuation.

It is many peoples opinion that fairy tales are too violent for childrens. I do not agree with this position. My grandparents' enjoyed reading aloud classic stories to my sister's and me. My sisters memorys of these read aloud times are all wonderful, they assure me. As for me, Red Riding Hoods demise at the wolves hands did not scare me at all. I could not wait to hear what happened to Hansel and Gretel after they got fat enough! A childs delight should not be measured in such black and white terms.

_____

_____

_____

_____

_____

_____

_____

_____

_____

_____

Name _____

1. Please finish the following sentences:

I see my mom putting ingredients in the pot. I see _____.

I see my sister making a sandwich. I see _____.

I see my little cousin tying his shoes. I see _____.

2. Complete the following sentence with three different observations. Try to use specific visual details to communicate what you see in your mind's eye.

I see my friend pouring the soda. I see

a. _____.

b. _____.

c. _____.

Extra Practice: Complete the following sentence with three different visual observations:

The policeman watched _____.

Name _____

Remember that *-le* and the consonant that comes before these letters form the last syllable of a word.

si**zzle**   ta**ble**

A. Choose an ending from the box to write a word that ends in a consonant + -le syllable.

ble	gle	tle	kle	dle

1. wad __ __ __

2. rum __ __ __

3. sprin __ __ __

4. wig __ __ __

5. hus __ __ __

B. Use the words from above to complete the story. Circle any other consonant + -le words that you find.

Duck, Worm, and Turtle were all outside on a bright, sunny day. "Aren't you hot with such a heavy shell?" Duck asked Turtle with a cackle.

"You resemble a rock," Worm said with a giggle. Then the clouds rolled in and the rain started to 6. _____ . The thunder began to

7. _____. Worm had to 8. _____ to a dry place. Duck had to 9. _____ to shelter. But Turtle did not need to 10. _____. He tucked his head into his shell and stayed dry right where he was.

A. Complete each sentence with a vocabulary word.

chameleon	rummaged	scrounging	pathetic
undetected	generosity	pursuing	famine

1. Many folk tale characters are known for their kindness and

   _____.

2. African folk tales often feature insect and animal characters, such as a

   spider or a _____.

3. My grandmother _____ through her attic to find her favorite

   book from her childhood.

4. At one point in the story, the children were so hungry they were

   _____ for food.

5. The children in the story were very brave, but the enemy was

   _____.

B. Write sentences of your own, using the remaining vocabulary words.

6. _____

   _____

7. _____

   _____

8. _____

   _____

Name _____

In stories and in real life, one event can make another event
occur. For example, if your alarm does not go off, then you might
be late for school. The first event is the **cause**, and the second
event is the **effect**. Authors use signal words or phrases such as
as a result, so, therefore, because, due to, and *then* to show the
relationships between events.

**Read the following article. Underline the signal words or phrases
that show the relationships between events. Then write the cause
and effect of each situation as indicated by the signal words.**

     Passing on traditions is very important to some families because they feel
it keeps family memories alive. When an older relative tells the story of his
father's immigration to America, he is passing on part of the family tradition.
Traditions also accompany holiday gatherings. Every year special events,
such as holiday dinners and celebrations, take place. As a result, familiarity
with the events is passed on to the younger generations. Then these
youngsters grow up and pass on their awareness of traditions. Therefore,
family tradition survives through the centuries.

1. cause _____

   effect _____

2. cause _____

_____

   effect _____

3. cause _____

   effect _____

_____

4. cause _____

   effect _____

_____

© Macmillan/McGraw-Hill

Name _____

As you read *The Magic Gourd*, fill in the Cause and Effect Chart.

Cause		Effect
	 →	
	→	
	→	
	→	
	→	
	→	

How does the information you wrote in this Cause and Effect Chart help
you make inferences and analyze the story structure of *The Magic Gourd*?

R 2.0 Reading Comprehension (Focus on Informational Materials)

As I read, I will pay attention to intonation.

	The Navajo (NAH-vah-hoh) Indians call themselves the
6	*Dineh* (dee-NAY). In Navajo, their name means "The People."
14	Over 255,000 Navajo live in the United States today. Their
23	nation is the largest in the country.
30	For generations, the Navajo have made beautiful weavings,
38	baskets, and jewelry. Their arts reflect their traditions, their
47	history, and their modern life.
52	Centuries ago, the Navajo settled in a part of the Southwest
63	now called the Four Corners. It's called that because the
73	borders of four states meet in one spot.
81	The Four Corners area has beautiful canyons, mesas, rivers,
90	and rock formations. But the high desert climate is harsh and
101	dry. Long ago, the Navajo lived in hogans. They moved often to find
112	grass for their sheep and horses. When the climate permitted,
122	they planted corn, squash, and melons. At times, on the brink
133	of **famine**, they had to be good farmers to get by.
144	In 1868, the United States and the Navajo signed a treaty.
154	The treaty promised them their own government, called the
163	Navajo Nation. The treaty also created the huge Navajo Reservation in
173	the Four Corners area. 177

Comprehension Check

1. How does the climate affect the Navajo? **Cause and Effect**

2. Why is art important to the Navajo? **Draw Conclusions**

	Words Read	–	Number of Errors	=	Words Correct Score
First Read		–		=	
Second Read		–		=	

CA **R 1.1** Read aloud narrative and expository text fluently and accurately
and with appropriate pacing, **intonation**, and expression.

Name _____

A **time line** organizes information chronologically, or in time order.
Time lines are divided into spans of years. The time moves from
the earliest on the left to the latest on the right. Events are listed
on the time line in the year they occurred.

Use the time line below to answer the questions.

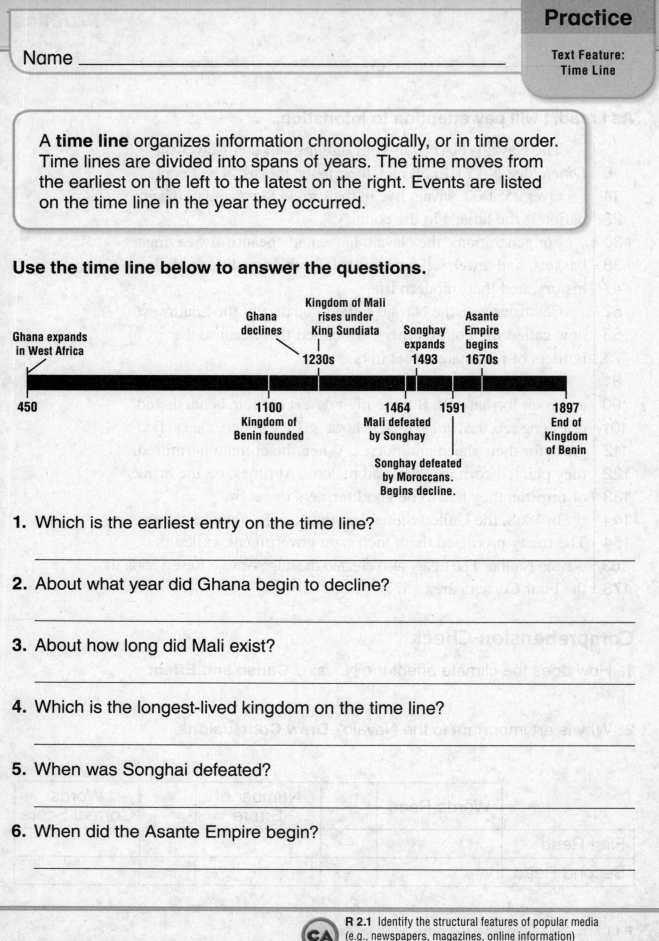

1. Which is the earliest entry on the time line?

_____

2. About what year did Ghana begin to decline?

_____

3. About how long did Mali exist?

_____

4. Which is the longest-lived kingdom on the time line?

_____

5. When was Songhai defeated?

_____

6. When did the Asante Empire begin?

_____

© Macmillan/McGraw-Hill

CA **R 2.1** Identify the structural features of popular media
(e.g., newspapers, magazines, online information)
and use the features to obtain information.

Name _____

When you read, you should use the context, or surrounding words, to help you determine the meaning of unfamiliar vocabulary. One kind of **context clue** is restatement, in which the meaning of a word is restated after the word appears. Look at the example:

The country was afflicted by famine. It suffered from an extreme scarcity of food.

The meaning of the word *famine* is restated in the sentence that follows it.

Read each sentence. Circle the word whose meaning is restated. Then write the meaning on the line.

1. Passing on cultural traditions is important to Malians, the people who live

   in Mali. _____

2. Often storytelling is accompanied by djembes, which are drums that people play as others tell stories, dance, or sing.

   _____

3. The Dogon, a tribe of people in Mali who live at the base of the Bandiagara Cliffs, have rituals of their own.

   _____

4. The Dama dance, which is religious, is part of the Dogon tradition.

   _____

5. Part of the Dama dance is done on stilts, which are long poles people can stand on to mimic the long legs of a water bird.

   _____

© Macmillan/McGraw-Hill

R 1.4 Monitor expository text for unknown words or words with novel meanings by using word, sentence, and paragraph clues to determine meaning.

The Magic Gourd • **Grade 6/Unit 2**   125

CA

Using the Word Study Steps

1. LOOK at the word.

2. SAY the word aloud.

3. STUDY the letters in the word.

4. WRITE the word.

5. CHECK the word.

   Did you spell the word right?

   If not, go back to step 1.

A. Add a consonant + *le* to each word to write a spelling word.

1. bicy___ ___ ___
2. squig___ ___ ___
3. dura___ ___ ___
4. mus___ ___ ___
5. scru___ ___ ___

6. noo___ ___ ___
7. whis___ ___ ___
8. scram___ ___ ___
9. sim___ ___ ___
10. bea___ ___ ___

B. The spelling words below are written backwards. Write them correctly.

11. elpmid _____
12. layor _____
13. elbbauqs _____
14. lanoitan _____
15. elbarucni _____

16. elttorht _____
17. elbaulav _____
18. elbaruces _____
19. elpurdauq _____
20. lavivrus _____

© Macmillan/McGraw-Hill

CA **LC 1.5** Spell frequently misspelled words correctly
(e.g., *their, they're, there*).

Name _____

A. Proofreading Activity

There are six spelling mistakes in the story below. Circle the misspelled words. Write the words correctly on the lines below.

Long ago, each animal in the village had only one kind of food to eat. It was enough for servial, but the animals grew tired of eating the same thing. "I can't eat another noodel," Spider declared. "I never want to scrambel another egg," Fox agreed. Rabbit was tired of eating carrots, so the three friends went to see Owl. Owl had a simpel plan. "If all four of us combine our food into a stew, we'll have quadrupal the food." The animals did as Owl suggested and had a royale feast.

1. _____ 3. _____ 5. _____

2. _____ 4. _____ 6. _____

B. Writing Activity

Imagine another problem the animals might have. Write a tale describing the problem the animals have and how they solve it. Use at least five spelling words.

_____

_____

_____

_____

_____

_____

_____

_____

_____

_____

_____

LC 1.5 Spell frequently misspelled words correctly
(e.g., *their, they're, there*).

- You can use an **appositive** to combine two short sentences in one.

Read each pair of sentences. Then combine them using an appositive word or phrase. Be sure to write the new sentence using a comma or commas to set off the appositive.

1. The serum was located in Anchorage. Anchorage is a city in southern Alaska.

   _____

   _____

2. Alfred John heard the roar of the steam engine. He was a five-year-old Athabaskan Indian.

   _____

   _____

3. Alfred wore his warmest shoes. They were caribou legskin boots.

   _____

   _____

4. Bill's dogsled team raced toward Tolovana. Tolovana was the first relay stop some fifty-two miles away.

   _____

   _____

5. Bill enjoyed his regular job. His regular job was transporting mail and freight with his dog team.

   _____

   _____

© Macmillan/McGraw-Hill

 LC 1.0 Written and Oral English Language Conventions

Name _____

- An **appositive** is a word or group of words that follows a noun and identifies or explains the noun.
- Commas are used to set off most appositives from the rest of the sentence.
- You can use an appositive to combine two short sentences.

Proofread this persuasive essay. Then rewrite the essay using appositives to combine sentences. Add any necessary commas. Correct any mistakes in capitalization or punctuation.

many dogs work hard every day. These Dogs are called service dogs. Our town has a program to train these animals. The program is called PAWS. PAWS dogs help not only people who are blind, but also those who are hearing impaired and those with paralyzed hands or legs. The dogs are trained to pick up objects open or close doors turn lights on and off and help the person get into and out of a wheelchair. Contact the organization to offer your support. You can help in two ways. You can volunteer your time. You can give funds.

_____
_____
_____
_____
_____
_____
_____
_____

Name _____

1. This is practice in SHOWING observations from different perspectives. Please read:

   A Long flight of stairs to the top of the building looks like _____.

      2. Finish this sentence from the following perspectives:

         a. A child:

         b. A grandparent:

         c. A baby:

         d. A man with a broken leg:

2. Pick one of the observers, underline it, and write three sentences describing an empty soda can from that perspective.

   _____

   _____

   _____

   _____

   _____

   _____

   _____

   _____

   _____

   _____

   _____

   _____

Extra Practice: Select a different observer: _____. Now, write three sentences from his/her perspective describing falling snow.

© Macmillan/McGraw-Hill

Name _____

When two vowels team up in a word, they stay in the same syllable.

s**ea**/w**ee**d   m**ai**n/t**ai**n   fr**ee**/dom

A. Add a vowel team syllable from the box to each syllable to form a word. Use the words to complete the story below.

| fair | plain | lead | gree | veal |

1. mis __ __ __ __

2. un __ __ __ __

3. a __ __ __ __

4. ex __ __ __ __ __

5. re __ __ __ __

I think most people will **6.** _____ that it is wise to be honest. It is **7.** _____ to **8.** _____ others. It may cause real harm. If you do something dishonest, the best thing to do is to **9.** _____ the truth. Then **10.** _____ that you will be honest in the future.

B. Now write three sentences telling about a time when you or someone you know did the right thing, even though it was difficult. Use words with the vowel teams *ea*, *ie*, *ee*, *ai*, *oa*, and *oo* in your sentences. Circle each word that has a vowel team syllable.

_____

_____

_____

Name _____

A. Fill in each blank with a vocabulary word.

flourish	foreman	employee	fulfill
gleefully	gloated	vigorously	deny

1. The cowboy knew they would not _____ him entry to the rodeo.

2. The man _____ about his special ability to lasso cattle.

3. The children _____ ran home so they could play outside.

4. The team practiced _____ all afternoon, and they were tired when they finished.

5. The new _____ reported directly to the manager of the company.

6. Grapes and oranges _____ in southern California.

7. Many boys hoped to _____ their dreams of becoming cowboys.

8. The _____ of the farm decides which crops will be picked next.

B. Choose two vocabulary words from the list above. Use them in sentences of your own.

9. _____

   _____

10. _____

   _____

© Macmillan/McGraw-Hill

 R 1.0 Word Analysis, Fluency, and Systematic Vocabulary Development

Name _____

Read the passage and answer the questions.

Before the American Southwest was American, Spanish and Mexican settlers made their homes in the places we now call Texas, New Mexico, Arizona, and southern California. Many descendants of these early settlers still remain. Ranching was the business to be in, and my relatives were *rancheros*, or ranch owners. My name is Hernando Arturo Castillo. When I was a boy, most of my nights were filled with adventure stories told around the campfire. My friends were the *gauchos*, Spanish for cowboys. That's all I ever wanted to be. Their lives seemed so daring, even though the work was hard. I never became a gaucho, partly because I tried it. When I was sixteen, I went with the gauchos on a cattle drive to the Northwest. Saying the work was hard was an understatement! I have never been so tired and scared as I was on those lonely plains at night. From that point on, I knew I would do better as a *ranchero*. I followed in my father's footsteps, much to his delight.

1. Where is the passage set? Why is the setting important?

_____

_____

_____

_____

_____

2. Who is the main character in the passage? Describe his perspective as he narrates his own story.

_____

_____

_____

_____

_____

© Macmillan/McGraw-Hill

As you read *Juan Verdades,* fill in the Character, Setting, Plot Chart

Characters	Setting	Plot

How does the information you wrote in this Character, Setting, Plot Chart
help you monitor comprehension of *Juan Verdades*?

R 2.0 Reading Comprehension (Focus on Informational Materials)

© Macmillan/McGraw-Hill

Name _____

As I read, I will pay attention to intonation and phrasing.

	If Benny Stone could see what lay ahead, he'd probably
10	be itching to get to Old Mesilla. Instead, he squirmed. The
21	car seat was hot and made him sweat more. His neck itched
33	and he wished he were back home.
40	His mom, however, was a different story. The farther they
50	got from Minneapolis, the lighter Benny's mother seemed.
58	It was as if she was shedding burdens onto the highway as
70	they traveled southwest, the convertible top pulled back.
78	Suddenly, she jabbed her finger at the windshield. "Look!
87	There it is!" In the backseat, Garcia, Benny's black Labrador
97	retriever, turned obediently, whipping himself in the face
105	with one wind-blown ear.
109	A large sign loomed on the side of the road. "Welcome
120	to New Mexico, the Land of Enchantment," Benny read
129	as it zoomed out of view. He had stopped complaining.
139	Seeing his mom all grinning and light was almost worth the
150	trip. Well, almost. He could still name about ten things he'd
161	rather do this summer than spend it with his mother in some
173	tiny southwestern town. 176

Comprehension Check

1. Why does Benny change his mind about New Mexico? **Character, Setting, Plot**

2. How do you think Benny's summer is going to turn out? **Make Predictions**

	Words Read	–	Number of Errors	=	Words Correct
First Read		–		=	
Second Read		–		=	

R 1.1 Read aloud narrative and expository text fluently and accurately and with appropriate pacing, **intonation**, and expression.

© Macmillan/McGraw-Hill

Name _____

Maps are used to show the features of an area. A map usually
has a compass rose to show you north/south orientation. A map
also has a scale to show the relationship between the distances
on the map and the actual distances between physical locations.

The map below shows some unusual place names in the western
United States.

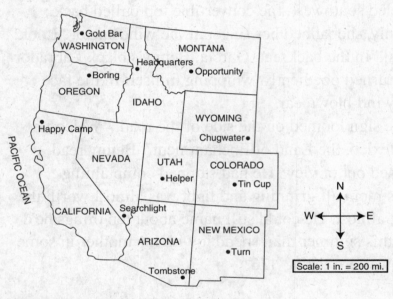

Use the map to answer the questions.

1. What does the map show?

_____

_____

2. In which state is Searchlight found? _____

3. Which city on the map is located in Montana? _____

4. Which state is north of Boring, Oregon? _____

5. Which city is about 400 miles west of Chugwater, Wyoming?

_____

© Macmillan/McGraw-Hill

CA R 2.1 Identify the structural features of popular media (e.g., newspapers,
magazines, online information) and use the features to obtain information.

Name _____

Words consist of a variety of parts: prefixes, base words, suffixes, and inflectional endings. **Base words** give the heart of a word's meaning. If you can identify and understand the base word, you can use your knowledge of its meaning to determine the meaning of a larger word.

Example: I hope to find a qualified <u>employee</u>.

The base of the word *employee* is *employ*, which means "use or work." The suffix *-ee* means "one who." Therefore, the word *employee* means "one who works."

A. Write each base word. Then write a definition of the whole word.

1. illness

Base word: _____

Definition: _____

_____

2. memorial

Base word: _____

Definition: _____

_____

3. novelty

Base word: _____

Definition: _____

_____

4. organization

Base word: _____

Definition: _____

_____

B. Choose two words from above. Use them in sentences of your own.

5. _____

_____

6. _____

_____

Name _____

Using the Word Study Steps

1. LOOK at the word.
2. SAY the word aloud.
3. STUDY the letters in the word.
4. WRITE the word.
5. CHECK the word.
   Did you spell the word right?
   If not, go back to step 1.

A. Find the Words

Find and circle the spelling word hidden in each set of letters. Then write it on the line provided.

1. e a r e q u a l i t y i v g s _____
2. r o a t e x p l o i t e n d f _____
3. s e e c e i l i n g i a n d _____
4. k r e a c r e a t u r e s _____
5. v o a t i p o i s o n o u s t e r _____
6. c o r f d s h o u l d e r y s _____
7. p e n m o i s t e n d e n t _____
8. g r e a p e d i g r e e n f p _____
9. s t r e a m l i n e c k s o n _____
10. p e a c w e a l t h y _____

B. Make a Puzzle

Make up a puzzle of your own using the space on this page. Give it to someone else to solve. Be sure to include at least five spelling words.

 LC 1.5 Spell frequently misspelled words correctly (e.g., *their, they're, there*).

Name _____

A. Proofreading Activity

There are six spelling mistakes in the story below. Circle the misspelled words. Write the words correctly on the lines below.

Once there was a young man who was in love with a wealthie farmer's daughter. The farmer didn't think anyone was good enough for his daughter. The young man said, "I may not have a fancy pedigrea, but I am a hard worker. I am helthy, and I love your daughter. That should be enough."

To prove himself, the young man would voluntear for the most difficult jobs on the farm. He bent over the fields until he could hardly straiten himself up. The farmer finally agreed to let the young man marry his daughter. The farmer said, "Men who are willing to *say* they love someone are common. Men who are willing to *show* they love someone are treazures. Welcome to the family!"

1. _____ 3. _____ 5. _____

2. _____ 4. _____ 6. _____

B. Writing Activity

Write a story about a time when you or someone you know showed honesty. Use at least four spelling words in your paragraph.

_____

_____

_____

_____

 LC 1.5 Spell frequently misspelled words correctly
(e.g., *their, they're, there*).

Juan Verdades • Grade 6/Unit 3   139

© Macmillan/McGraw-Hill

Name _____

• An indirect object is a noun or pronoun in the predicate that answers the question *to whom?* or *for whom?* or *to what?* or *for what?* after an **action verb**.

Underline each action verb once and each direct object twice.
Put brackets [ ] around each indirect object.

1. Mr. Wagner gave Jose some lessons.

2. Mrs. Wagner baked everybody cookies.

3. Jose read his sister a story.

4. His sister sang Jose a song.

5. Jose's grandfather gave him some good advice.

6. Jose sent his mother a birthday card.

7. She gave him her thanks.

8. Mr. Wagner bought his daughter a violin.

9. She showed us her violin.

10. Jose handed Mrs. Wagner a red rose.

11. Jose played his grandfather music.

12. Schools give music students excellent opportunities.

 LC 1.0 Written and Oral English Language Conventions

- An **action verb** is a word that expresses action. It tells what the subject does or did.
- A direct object is a noun or pronoun that receives the action of the verb. It answers the question *what*? or *whom*? after the verb.
- An indirect object is a noun or pronoun in the predicate that answers *to whom*? or *for whom*? or *to what*? after an action verb. An indirect always comes before a direct object.

Rewrite the character sketch below, correcting any mistakes made with verbs that do not agree with their subjects.

Jose's grandfather are always telling him stories about old New Mexico. Popi are a small man, thin and wiry. He has unusually large hands, though, the fingers thick and blunt. He wear heavy black glasses with thick plastic lenses. His eyes is pale brown, almost yellow-gold. Popi come from Mexico, and although his English seem perfect, he speak with a faint accent, almost as if he are singing. Popi often sing Jose songs from Mexico.

_____
_____
_____
_____
_____
_____
_____
_____
_____
_____

Name _____

1. Read the following sentences:

   My coin had slipped through the crack.

   My alarm clock never went off.

   I felt like I was going crazy.

2. Think of each of these sentences as a CAUSE. Now write a second sentence for each of these sentences that shows the EFFECT that this event had or WHAT HAPPENED NEXT.

Example: My coin had slipped through the crack. I quickly tore the cushions off the sofa to find it.

_____

_____

_____

_____

_____

_____

_____

_____

_____

_____

_____

_____

Extra Practice: Try this activity again using the following sentences.

   The door slammed in my face.

   I ripped the wrapping paper off the present.

   I threw the ball to Ruby as hard as I could.

© Macmillan/McGraw-Hill

CA W 1.0 Writing Strategies

> Every vowel can stand for the /ə/ sound in English. You can hear the /ə/ sound spelled *a* in *about,* spelled *u* in *minute,* spelled *e* in *happen,* spelled *o* in *gallop,* and spelled *i* in *direct.* Sometimes the /ə/ sound is followed by *r* at the end of a word and stands for the /ər/ sound. For example: ***teacher, doctor, caterpillar.***

A. Read the sentences. Write the words that have the final /ər/ sound on the line.

1. A writer needs time to think of good subjects. _____

2. Stories are often similar to real life. _____

3. An author can be seen as a messenger. _____

4. He or she teaches lessons through specific subject matter.

   _____

5. Sometimes writing is turned into a show for the television viewer.

   _____

6. Directors, producers, and actors all play a part in bringing us

   entertainment. _____

7. They also deliver messages to the audience. _____

8. Creators of stories play an important role in society. _____

B. Choose two of the words that have the /ər/ sound and use each in a sentence.

9. _____

   _____

10. _____

   _____

Complete the crossword puzzle with words from the vocabulary list using the clues below.

| coincidences | sweeten | phase | hobbled |
| sheepishly | prospered | sumptuous | devoted |

Across

1. extremely rich and magnificent
4. walked unsteadily
6. a part of something that changes
7. accidental events that seem to be connected

Down

1. to make more attractive
2. in an embarrassed manner
3. succeeded
5. feeling strong affection or attachment

© Macmillan/McGraw-Hill

 R 1.0 Word Analysis, Fluency, and Systematic Vocabulary Development

Read the passage and answer the questions.

"The Bear and the Two Travelers"
A Fable by Aesop

Two men were traveling together, when a bear suddenly met them on their path. One of the men quickly climbed into a tree and concealed himself in the branches. The other, seeing that he would be attacked, fell flat on the ground. When the bear came up and nudged him with his snout, and smelled him all over, the man held his breath and feigned the appearance of death as well as he could. The bear soon left him, for it is said bears will not touch a dead body. When the bear was quite gone, the other traveler descended from the tree, and jocularly inquired of his friend what the bear had whispered in his ear. "He gave me this advice," his companion replied. "Never travel with a friend who deserts you at the approach of danger."

Moral: Misfortune tests the sincerity of friends.

1. What problem do the two travelers encounter at the beginning?

_____

2. How do the travelers react to the situation?

_____

3. What problem arises for the second traveler?

_____

_____

4. Relate the moral of the story in your own words.

_____

Name _____

As you read *Rumpelstiltskin's Daughter*, fill in the
Problem and Solution Chart.

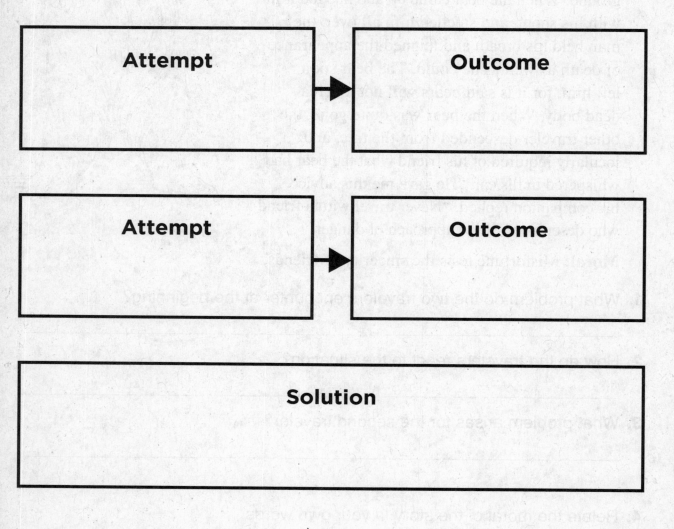

Problem

Attempt → **Outcome**

Attempt → **Outcome**

Solution

How does the information you wrote in this Problem and Solution Chart
help you better understand *Rumpelstiltskin's Daughter*?

 R 2.0 Reading Comprehension (Focus on Informational Materials)

As I read, I will pay attention to pacing.

	Long ago in a land of forests and mountains, two kingdoms sat
12	side by side. One, on the borders of a forest, was inhabited by men
26	and women who lived and worked on farms and in villages. In this
39	place, the sun shone on most days and rain fell only when it was
53	really needed. As any traveler through the region could report, the
64	people there were always busy, usually happy, and never sad for
75	long.
76	The second kingdom, however, was hidden from sight. For it lay
87	mostly beneath a mountain whose base went so deep that it seemed
99	to reach almost to the fiery center of the earth. This was the
112	kingdom of the gnomes, and its ruler was one Beryl Hardstone.
123	Beryl was a princely sort, given his fabulous wealth. Beryl had
134	all the traits and powers of gnomes. He was small, bearded, and not
147	particularly handsome, at least in human terms. He could move
157	through solid earth as easily as through air. And he could carry
169	with him whatever he held in his hands. This was useful because,
181	in true gnome fashion, Beryl was a miner and he liked to take his
195	precious stones with him. 199

Comprehension Check

1. Why does the author compare the two kingdoms? **Author's Purpose**

2. What can you infer about the citizens who live in the second kingdom? **Make Inferences**

	Words Read	–	Number of Errors	=	Words Correct Score
First Read		–		=	
Second Read		–		=	

© Macmillan/McGraw-Hill

CA **R 1.1** Read aloud narrative and expository text fluently and accurately and with appropriate **pacing**, intonation, and expression.

Name _____

A **myth** is a story that explains occurrences in nature through the intervention of gods and goddesses.

A **moral** is a practical lesson contained in the narrative.

Hyperbole is the deliberate use of exaggeration for emphasis. Myths sometimes use hyperbole to describe human weaknesses.

Now that you have read *Rumpelstiltskin's Daughter*, you know how myths use hyperbole, explain natural occurrences, and teach a moral at the same time. Think of an explanation for a natural occurrence. Write your own myth about this occurrence. You can make up gods and goddesses, or you can borrow them from ancient cultures. Be sure that your myth not only explains an occurrence but also teaches a lesson, such as "It doesn't pay to be greedy" or "Be kind to everyone."

_____

_____

_____

_____

_____

_____

_____

_____

_____

_____

_____

_____

 R 3.7 Explain the effects of common literary devices (e.g., symbolism, imagery, metaphor) in a variety of fictional and nonfictional texts.

An **idiom** is an expression whose meaning cannot necessarily be understood from the meanings of its idnividual words When you read an idiom, use the context of the sentence or paragraph to help you identify its meaning. Often, the dictionary will provide an entry that explains how a popular idiom is used.

Example: The salesman needs to sell the last television on the floor. He might *sweeten the pot* by offering a free three-year warranty.

A. Underline the idiom in each sentence. Write what it means in the space provided. If you have trouble, consult a dictionary.

1. I tried to break the ice by telling the group a story.

   _____

2. When I forgot the ending, my older brother said, "That's par for the course. He can never remember a thing."

   _____

3. My brother is on the ball. He is always prepared.

   _____

4. When I turned in the first draft of my report, the teacher said she wanted to make sure I was on the right track.

   _____

5. My mom bends over backwards to get us to our school functions. She sometimes even misses her book-club meetings to take us to ball practice.

   _____

B. Write a sentence that contains an idiomatic expression.

6. _____

   _____

   _____

Using the Word Study Steps

1. LOOK at the word.
2. SAY the word aloud.
3. STUDY the letters in the word.
4. WRITE the word.
5. CHECK the word. Did you spell the word right? If not, go back to step 1.

Crossword Puzzle

Use the clues to complete the puzzle.

ACROSS

1. Eva enjoyed the soup but felt it had too much _____.

6. Mr. Change brought over a _____ of trout.

7. I wish I could play field hockey, but I'm only an _____.

DOWN

2. When she told on her sister, Amy felt like a _____.

3. Mr. Sims is a great _____ on Broadway.

4. The soup had more _____ when Mrs. Martinez added spices.

5. Being a _____ at the 90th Street Café would be an interesting job.

© Macmillan/McGraw-Hill

LC 1.5 Spell frequently misspelled words correctly (e.g., *their, they're, there*).

A. Proofreading Activity

There are five spelling mistakes in the paragraph below. Circle the misspelled words. Write the words correctly on the lines below.

   Interesting events happen at the most unlikely of times. Watching the street on a boring day can prove to be one of the most entertaining events. Try to be a careful serobver. You never know who will walk by. The neighborhood ackter may erdanw by rehearsing a monologue. The wayter from the local restaurant may run across the street to the deli to stock up on extra vineger. The daily activities of those in your neighborhood can often be quite unusual and exciting.

1. _____   3. _____   5. _____

2. _____   4. _____

B. Writing Activity

Think about a time when something unusual happened that you didn't expect. Write a paragraph about that particular day. Use five spelling words.

_____

_____

_____

_____

_____

_____

_____

_____

LC 1.5 Spell frequently misspelled words correctly (e.g., *their, they're, there*).

Rumpelstiltskin's Daughter
Grade 6/Unit 3   151

© Macmillan/McGraw-Hill

Name _____

- A verb in the **past tense** tells about an action that already happened.
- Add **-ed** to most verbs to show the past tense.
- A verb in the **future tense** tells about an action that is going to happen.
- To write about the future, use the special verb **will**.

A. Write the verb in parentheses in the past tense.

1. Eva (want) something exciting to happen on her street.

   _____

2. A whole week (pass) with nothing for her to do.

   _____

3. Eva's friend (whisper) to her that someone was coming to visit.

   _____

4. Eva (dress) up in her best outfit.

   _____

5. Her friend (warn) Eva not to get too excited.

   _____

6. Eva (hope) that something would happen soon.

   _____

B. Change the following verbs into the future tense.

7. like _____

8. enjoy _____

9. pick _____

10. make _____

11. remove _____

12. build _____

© Macmillan/McGraw-Hill

 LC 1.0 Written and Oral English Language Conventions

Name _____

- A verb in the **present tense** tells what happens now.
- In the present tense, you must have **subject-verb agreement.** Add **-s** to most verbs if the subject is singular. Do not add **-s** if the subject is plural or **I** or **you**.
- A verb in the **past tense** tells about an action that already happened.
- Add **-ed** to most verbs to show past tense.
- A verb in the **future tense** tells about an action that is going to happen.
- To write about the future, use the special verb **will**.

The writer of this dialogue did not proofread for mistakes. Put brackets [ ] around any incorrect verb tenses. Rewrite the dialogue correcting verb forms and adding correct punctuation.

Juliet and Romeo were sitting at the library table.

Juliet said Don't look at my journal, Romeo

I was not looking cry Romeo

Yes, you were I sees you cry Juliet

Romeo whispers keeps your voice down

I'm only trying to puts my thoughts and feelings into writing whisper Juliet

Go right ahead say Romeo

Juliet replied Thank you. I do just that

_____

_____

_____

_____

_____

_____

_____

Name _____

The Game

by: Trevor Brown

The game ended and everybody went home. I spent the rest of the night thinking about that last play. "Don't shoot it!" Kwame yelled. "I can make it!" I called. Before the game started, I never thought I would have the ball for the last shot. The next day, coach told me what happened was okay.

1. Read the paragraph above.

2. Rewrite this paragraph in your journals and experiment with the order of the sentences in order to create tension. Remember, the more tension and conflict you can build at the beginning of your writing, the more interested a reader will be to find out what happens.

Example: You can use the example below to help you figure out what to do. Notice that the sentences in the 2 paragraphs are the same, but the order of the sentences has changed.

Passage 1:

Art class turned out to be fun today. When the teacher saw my work, she said, "See? I knew you could do it." I ended up making a mask that I really liked. Before art class, I was so nervous I could barely speak.

Passage 2:

Before art class, I was so nervous I could barely speak. I ended up making a mask that I really liked. When the teacher saw my work, she said, "See? I knew you could do it." Art class turned out to be fun today.

Extra Practice: Write 3-5 sentences about an experience that you had yesterday. Then rewrite your paragraph by changing the order of the sentences, but not the sentences themselves.

_____

_____

_____

_____

© Macmillan/McGraw-Hill

 CA **W 1.0** Writing Strategies

There are some words in the English language that are frequently misspelled. Use your knowledge of sounds and spelling patterns to learn these commonly misspelled words.

For each number below, circle the correctly spelled word and then use it in a sentence.

1. freind   hurd   beautiful   beleive

_____

2. led   cheif   beggining   sence

_____

_____

3. speach   nife   grive   meant

_____

_____

4. paid   flys   feerce   speack

_____

_____

5. sceene   although   croud   bilt

_____

_____

A. Write the vocabulary word that best completes each sentence.

bewildering   moderate   hamper   prohibit   accessible

1. Many people make medium or _____ donations to their favorite charities every year.

2. Some people find it _____ when they are faced with complicated and confusing instructions.

3. Making aid _____ to those who need it is often the job of relief organizations.

4. By giving her time, Cynthia hopes to help, not _____, the patients' progress.

5. Some organizations may _____ young people from volunteering, but others are happy to have young volunteers.

B. Write sentences using each one of the vocabulary words.

6. _____

_____

7. _____

_____

8. _____

_____

9. _____

_____

10. _____

_____

© Macmillan/McGraw-Hill

R 1.0 Word Analysis, Fluency, and Systematic Vocabulary Development

Read the passage and answer the questions.

Helping others is easy to do. From opening a door for a stranger to volunteering at a local hospital, there are many ways to help others. When you are deciding how you want to help, it is important to find the volunteer work that is right for you. If you like working with people, you might volunteer at the hospital or at a nursing home. Usually these volunteer positions allow you time to visit with people, bring them flowers, tell them stories, and just provide company. If you like working with animals, you might volunteer at an animal shelter. There you might walk dogs, clean cages, or help with adoptions. Most of your time will be spent with animals, not humans. If you like working outdoors, you might volunteer with the park service. There you might plant flowers, rake leaves, or clean up litter. However you decide to help, your time will be well spent.

1. How are the three different volunteer positions alike?

   _____

   _____

2. What is the difference between volunteering at an animal shelter and volunteering at a hospital? _____

   _____

   _____

3. How is volunteering with the park service different from volunteering at the hospital? _____

   _____

   _____

4. How is volunteering for the animal shelter different from volunteering for the park service?

   _____

   _____

CA **R 2.2** Analyze text that uses the compare-and-contrast organizational pattern.

Name _____

As you read *Saving Grace*, fill in the Venn Diagram.

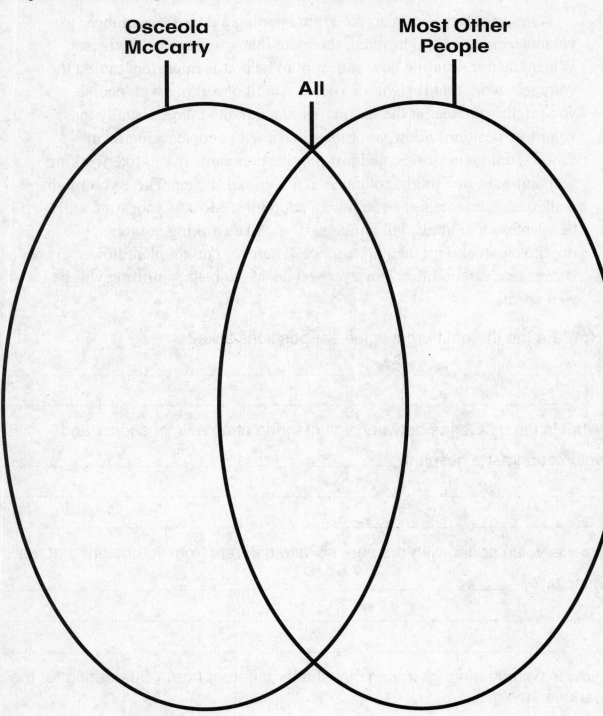

Osceola
McCarty

All

Most Other
People

© Macmillan/McGraw-Hill

How does the information you wrote in this Venn Diagram help you make
inferences and analyze *Saving Grace*?

CA R 2.2 Analyze text that uses the compare-and-contrast organizational
pattern.

Name _____

As I read, I will pay attention to pacing.

	Mary was the fifteenth of seventeen McLeod children.
8	She was one of the few born into freedom. Young Mary
19	worked the cotton and corn fields. She learned the value of
30	hard work, yet she was unsatisfied. She saw the opportunities
40	that the white children had. They went to school while she
51	worked. Mary ached for a better life.
58	Mary's mother worked for a white family. One day,
67	Mary went into the playhouse where the children did their
77	schoolwork. When Mary began to look at a book, one of
88	the girls took it away from her. She said that Mary couldn't
100	read, so she couldn't have that book. Instead she handed
110	Mary a picture book. With a heavy heart, Mary looked at the
122	pictures. After a while, her hurt hardened into a fierce
132	resolve. She *would* learn to read. No one could stop her.
143	After the Civil War, there were still two worlds in the
154	South. Education was not accessible to everyone. Many
162	whites did not think that blacks needed to read or write. But
174	Mary knew that she must learn to read to get a better life. 187

Comprehension Check

1. How was Mary McLeod's life different compared to the white children's? **Compare and Contrast**

2. What does Mary think she must do to have a better future? **Draw Conclusions**

	Words Read	−	Number of Errors	=	Words Correct Score
First Read		−		=	
Second Read		−		=	

R 1.1 Read aloud narrative and expository text fluently and accurately and with appropriate **pacing**, intonation, and expression.

© Macmillan/McGraw-Hill

Name _____

A book has different parts. These parts can be used to find information in the book.

A **title page** is the first page and tells the title, the author, and the publisher.

A **copyright page** tells when the book was written, who holds the copyright, and where the book was published.

A **table of contents** lists the names of the units, chapters, or other sections of the book with the page numbers.

A **glossary** defines difficult or specific terms used in the text.

An **index** is an alphabetical list of all the topics covered in the book with all the corresponding page numbers.

Answer the questions.

1. Where would you look to find the author's name? _____

2. Where would you look to find the meaning of an unfamiliar word?

    _____

3. Where would you look for the beginning page number of Chapter 5?

    _____

4. Where can you find out who published the book?

    _____

5. In a book about volunteering, where would you look to find information

    about a historic event? _____

6. Explain why the different parts of a book can help you write a report.

    _____

    _____

    _____

© Macmillan/McGraw-Hill

 R 2.0 Reading Comprehension (Focus on Informational Materials)

Name _____

Compare/Contrast Writing Frame

A. Summarize Saving Grace. Use the Compare/Contrast Writing Frame below.

Both Oseola McCarty's early years and later years are the **same** in some ways. They are the same because _____

_____

_____

_____ .

However, in other ways Oseola McCarty's early years and later years are **different**. They are different because _____

_____

_____ .

So, Oseola McCarty's early years and later years have both **similarities** and **differences**.

B. Rewrite the completed summary on another sheet of paper. Keep it as a model for writing a summary of an article or selection using this text structure.

 R 2.0 Reading Comprehension

Homographs are words that have the same spelling. However, homographs have different definitions and, sometimes, different pronunciations. For example, *sow* (rhymes with *go*) means "to plant seeds." *Sow* (rhymes with *now*) means "a female pig." Sometimes the word is stressed on different syllables. *Object* is stressed on the first syllable when it means a thing. It is stressed on the second syllable when it means to oppose something.

Definitions are provided for the homographs. Write a sentence for each definition of the word. The sentence should make the meaning clear.

1. project: something you are working on

_____

2. project: put forth or present

_____

3. dove: a kind of bird

_____

4. dove: past tense of dive

_____

5. wind: steady gusts of air

_____

6. wind: wrap around

_____

7. lead: make the way or go first

_____

8. lead: a metal

_____

© Macmillan/McGraw-Hill

Practice

Spelling:
Frequently Misspelled
Words

Name _____

Using the Word Study Steps

1. LOOK at the word.

2. SAY the word aloud.

3. STUDY the letters in the word.

4. WRITE the word.

5. CHECK the word.
   Did you spell the word right?
   If not, go back to step 1.

Find the Words

Find and circle the spelling words hidden in each set of letters. Then write the word on the line that follows.

1. w a i l g w a d d r e s s a m d s l s _____

2. a g a i n s t a w k i b g r u a t _____

3. w a l w a y s i c g e n t _____

4. p l a n s w e r a w o z k _____

5. e b b e c a u s e n x i q g _____

6. b e l i e v e a t o u t a v k _____

7. w a j k e r b r o u g h t o u r h _____

8. i n c h i l d r e n a d e h _____

9. t u l l p r c o u s i n i c k w d _____

10. d e d ' n t d o e s n ' t a i r ' n t _____

11. w a l f e d o l l a r i n y b i a r _____

12. e n o u g h i n w e d a d g r e _____

13. f r e c j e d u g u e s s _____

14. i n s t e a d o c n r i k h t _____

15. p i r w p i p e p e o p l e d _____

LC 1.5 Spell frequently misspelled words correctly
(e.g., *their, they're, there*).

Name _____

A. There are six spelling mistakes in the paragraph below. Circle the misspelled words. Then write the words correctly on the lines below.

    Charles allways wanted create a puppet theater, in which he controlled a puppet show. His couzin, Jake, didn't beleive he could do it, however. Charles said that other chilren would come to watch him perform. But Jake said he wouldn't get enuff people to come by. It seemed like Jake was always aganst him.

1. _____   2. _____

3. _____   4. _____

5. _____   6. _____

B. Writing Activity

Continue writing the story. Use at least four more spelling words.

_____

_____

_____

_____

_____

_____

_____

_____

LC 1.5 Spell frequently misspelled words correctly
(e.g., *their, they're, there*).

Name _____

The **present perfect** tense is used when the time period is not complete, is not mentioned, or is recent. It is also used with *for* and *since*.

The **past perfect** tense is used when two events took place in the past. The past perfect tense shows which event took place first.

The **future perfect** tense is used to describe an action that will take place, in the future, but before another action.

A. Use the present perfect form of each verb in a sentence.

1. I see (two movies this week) _____

_____

2. You pass (the test) _____

3. She arrives (recently from town) _____

4. Mark lives (here for four years) _____

_____

5. Yolanda works (here since 2004) _____

_____

B. Use the past perfect form to complete each sentence.

6. By the time we arrived, the food (eaten). _____

7. When she landed, the airport (closed). _____

C. Use the future perfect form to complete each sentence.

8. When we get there, she (wait) _____ for three hours.

9. By the time you arrive in France, Monique (learn) _____
to speak French more clearly.

10. By next Tuesday, you (spend) _____ four days working
on this project.

CA LC 1.2 Identify and properly use indefinite pronouns and present perfect, past perfect, and future perfect verb tenses; ensure that verbs agree with compound subjects.

The **present perfect** tense is used when the time period is not complete, is not mentioned, or is recent. It is also used with *for* and *since*.
The **past perfect** tense is used when two events took place in the past. The past perfect tense shows which event took place first.
The **future perfect** tense is used to describe an action that will take place in the future, but before another action.

Proofread this passage. Then rewrite the passage using the correct verb tenses.

Marcus had lived in the area since 1974. No one can believe he has spend so much time here. By the time he arrived, he had lives in almost every part of the country. But this is his favorite place, he says. He just doesn't want to move. But one day his daughter came to town, and she explained that he has to leave. He will have to move in with her someday, so that she can take care of him. By the time he leaves, he will has lived in every single region of this country.

_____

_____

_____

_____

_____

_____

_____

_____

_____

© Macmillan/McGraw-Hill

LC 1.2 Identify and properly use indefinite pronouns and present perfect, past perfect, and future perfect verb tenses; ensure that verbs agree with compound subjects.

Name _____

Writing Rubric

4 Excellent	3 Good	2 Fair	1 Unsatisfactory
Ideas and Content/ Genre	Ideas and Content/ Genre	Ideas and Content/ Genre	Ideas and Content/ Genre
Organization and Focus	Organization and Focus	Organization and Focus	Organization and Focus
Sentence Structure/ Fluency	Sentence Structure/ Fluency	Sentence Structure/ Fluency	Sentence Structure/ Fluency
Conventions	Conventions	Conventions	Conventions
Word Choice	Word Choice	Word Choice	Word Choice
Voice	Voice	Voice	Voice
Presentation	Presentation	Presentation	Presentation

© Macmillan/McGraw-Hill

CA **W 1.0** Writing Strategies

A **prefix** is a syllable that comes at the beginning of a word. It usually changes the meaning of the base word or the root.

If you do not know what the prefix of a word means, try to think of another word with the same prefix. You may not know what supergravity is, but you probably know what a superhero is. You can apply the meaning of *super* (*over and above*, *larger*) to the new word.

A. Underline each prefix in the words below. Write a meaning for the prefix.

1. provide _____   4. illegal _____

2. review _____   5. ungrateful _____

3. tricycle _____   6. disgrace _____

B. Use four of the words above in sentences of your own.

7. _____

_____

8. _____

_____

9. _____

_____

10. _____

_____

© Macmillan/McGraw-Hill

CA R 1.0 Word Analysis, Fluency, and Systematic Vocabulary Development

Name _____

Use the vocabulary words from the box and the clues below to solve the crossword puzzle.

grimaced	participate	ordeals	anticipated
dejectedly	encounter	nourishing	victorious

Across

3. made a facial expression of disgust

6. nutritious

7. severe trials or experiences

8. with sadness

Down

1. take part

2. having won

4. a meeting between people

5. expected

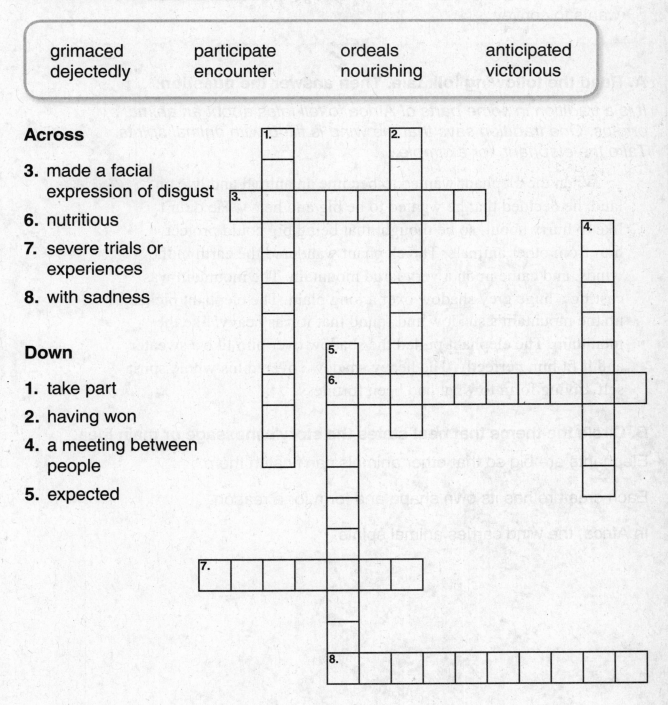

The theme is the overall idea or message the author of a story wants to convey.

A. Read the following folk tale. Then answer the question.

It is a tradition in some parts of Africa to tell tales about an animal's origins. One tradition says that the wind is filled with animal spirits. Take the elephant, for example.

When the elephant wanted to become an animal and live on land, he decided that he wanted to be big and heavy. He didn't like to hurry about, so he thought that being big could protect him from other animals. The elephant wandered the earth in the winds, and came upon a very large mountain. The mountain was casting a huge grey shadow over a long plain. The elephant picked up the mountain's shadow and found that it was heavy, like the mountain. The elephant pulled the shadow over him like a sweater and it fit him perfectly. The heavy shadow covered his whole spirit self, giving form to what had been formless.

B. Circle the theme that best states the story's message or main idea.

Elephants are big so that other animals can't catch them.

Each creature has its own shape and form for a reason.

In Africa, the wind carries animal spirits.

© Macmillan/McGraw-Hill

 R 3.6 Identify and analyze features of themes conveyed through characters, actions, and images.

Name _____

As you read *Ta-Na-E-Ka*, fill in the Theme Chart.

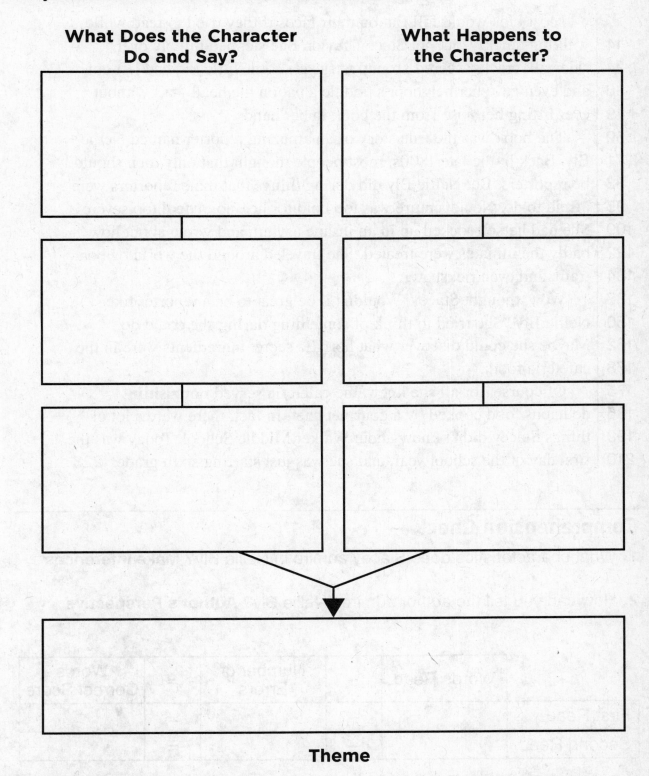

**What Does the Character
Do and Say?**

**What Happens to
the Character?**

Theme

 R 3.6 Identify and analyze features of themes conveyed through
characters, actions, and images.

As I read, I will pay attention to expression.

	Most kids would fall flat on their faces if they tried to read while
14	walking quickly, but not Stacey Taylor. She stepped nimbly over
24	sidewalk cracks, veered around a tricycle some little kid had left out,
36	and even gave her neighbor's poodle a pat on the head—all without
49	ever lifting her nose from the book in her hands.
59	The book was the true story of an amazing reporter named Nellie
71	Bly. Back in the late 1800s, most people thought that only men should
83	be reporters. But Nellie Bly did daring things that male reporters were
95	afraid to do. No adventure was too bold for her, no **ordeal** too severe.
109	She had herself locked up in an insane asylum and wrote about how
122	badly the inmates were treated. She traveled around the world by boat,
134	train, and even rickshaw.
138	Wow, thought Stacey. Wouldn't it be great to be a reporter like
150	Nellie Bly? She tried to think of something daring she could do.
162	Maybe she could discover what horrific secret ingredients were in the
173	cafeteria food.
175	Of course, for all she knew, the cafeteria served **nourishing**,
185	delicious food cooked by a gourmet chef. In fact, there were a lot of
199	things Stacey didn't know about Walker Middle School. Today was the
210	first day of the school year, and she was just starting sixth grade. 223

Comprehension Check

1. What characteristics does Stacey admire in Nellie Bly? **Make Inferences**

2. How can you tell the author admires Nellie Bly? **Author's Perspective**

	Words Read	–	Number of Errors	=	Words Correct Score
First Read		–		=	
Second Read		–		=	

© Macmillan/McGraw-Hill

R 1.1 Read aloud narrative and expository text fluently and accurately and with appropriate pacing, intonation, and **expression**.

Name _____

A fable is a short story that teaches a moral, often through the actions of animals that act like people.

A **moral** is a lesson taught by a fable or story. It is usually stated outright at the end of the fable.

Personification is a literary device where animals or things have human characteristics.

Read the fable and answer the questions.

The Ant and the Chrysalis

An Ant was running around in the sunshine looking for food when he came across a Chrysalis (the pupa stage of a butterfly) that was very near to changing. "Poor, pathetic animal!" cried the Ant with scorn. "What a sad fate is yours! While I can run all over the place, you lie here in your shell, unable to move." The Chrysalis heard all this, but did not make any reply. A few days later, the Ant felt himself shaded and fanned by the gorgeous wings of a beautiful Butterfly. "Behold in me," said the Butterfly, "your much-pitied friend! Boast now of your powers to run and climb as long as you can get me to listen."

Moral: *"Appearances are deceptive."*

1. Who are the main characters in the story? _____

_____

2. Why does the ant think the chrysalis is pathetic? _____

_____

3. How are the ant and the butterfly like people? _____

_____

4. What is the moral of the story? _____

5. Why was the ant wrong to pity the chrysalis? _____

_____

© Macmillan/McGraw-Hill

Many English words have **Latin roots**. Familiarizing yourself
with Latin root meanings will help you determine the meanings of
English words. These roots usually do not stand alone as words.

The Latin root *ject* means "to throw." In the word *dejectedly*, the
root means "put down" or "thrown down," as in *depressed*.

**A. Fill in the chart with as many words as possible that have the
Latin roots as listed. Use a dictionary if needed.**

1. *ject*: throw	2. *spect*: view	3. *scribe, script*: write, writing	4. *duc, duct*: lead

**B. Choose six of the words you listed above and use them in
sentences. Use at least one of the words in each sentence.**

5. _____

6. _____

7. _____

8. _____

9. _____

10. _____

© Macmillan/McGraw-Hill

(CA) **R 1.0** Word Analysis, Fluency, and Systematic Vocabulary Development

Name _____

Using the Word Study Steps

1. LOOK at the word.
2. SAY the word aloud.
3. STUDY the letters in the word.
4. WRITE the word.
5. CHECK the word.
   Did you spell the word right?
   If not, go back to step 1.

A. Alphabetical Order

Write the spelling words in alphabetical order.

1. _____   11. _____
2. _____   12. _____
3. _____   13. _____
4. _____   14. _____
5. _____   15. _____
6. _____   16. _____
7. _____   17. _____
8. _____   18. _____
9. _____   19. _____
10. _____   20. _____

B. Write the Words

Use the lines below to practice writing the spelling words.

_____ _____ _____ _____

_____ _____ _____ _____

_____ _____ _____ _____

LC 1.5 Spell roots, suffixes, prefixes, contractions, and
syllable constructions correctly.

Ta-Na-E-Ka • **Grade 6/Unit 3** 175

Name _____

A. Proofreading Activity

There are five spelling mistakes in the paragraph below. Circle the misspelled words. Write the words correctly on the lines below.

Upon discovery of some unnown artifacts, the town put together a team to uncover the historical significance of their find. Many independant scientists teamed together to untangal the mysteries of the ancient pieces. There was incredable joy when the scientists began to uncover facts about the pieces they discovered. The lead scientist even became a suparstar in the community for his contributions to the project.

1. _____   3. _____   5. _____

2. _____   4. _____

B. Writing Activity

Write a story about discovering an historical object, perhaps one you found in an attic or basement that revealed something you didn't know about your family. Use five spelling words.

_____

_____

_____

_____

_____

_____

_____

_____

Name _____

- A **predicate noun** follows a **linking verb** and renames or identifies the subject.
- A **predicate adjective** follows a linking verb and describes the subject.

In the space provided, write the predicate noun or predicate adjective in the following sentences. Also, identify the word as either a predicate noun or a predicate adjective.

1. The archaeologists felt happy.

   _____

2. Terracotta soldiers were the work of people in northern China.

   _____

3. The soldiers are a source of information for historians.

   _____

4. The soldiers seem real.

   _____

5. The men who created them are gone.

   _____

6. Their names are unknown.

   _____

7. The archaeologists could become prize winners.

   _____

8. The soldiers are a reminder of past glory.

   _____

9. Every soldier looks different.

   _____

10. They are truly works of art.

    _____

Name _____

- A **linking verb** does not show action. It links the subject to a noun or an adjective in the predicate.
- Common linking verbs are *am, is, are, was, were, be, being, been, seem, feel, appear, become, look, taste, smell.*

The writer of this short story did not proofread for mistakes. Rewrite the story, correcting any mistakes made with linking verbs.

Lee, a young archaeologist, was work on an important site in northern China. It was his first dig, and he was nervous. The dean of the school of archaeology was watched him carefully. The dean was expect Lee to make a big mistake. Lee, however, was very careful. One morning, when Lee had already be digging for hours, his tiny shovel hit something solid. Lee know immediately that it is not stone. He gingerly lifted the piece from the sand. It are an arm band, an exquisite piece of gold jewelry. Lee stand up carefully, hold his prize, and heading for the dean's tent.

_____

_____

_____

_____

_____

_____

_____

_____

_____

_____

_____

_____

© Macmillan/McGraw-Hill

 LC 1.0 Written and Oral English Language Conventions

Name _____

1. Read the following 2 unrelated sentences:

    Alex was running through the field.

    Alex said hi to his cousin.

2. Now, write a transition sentence or phrase that connects the two sentences and makes the events clear to the reader.

Example:

   Alex was running through the field.

   He accidentally tripped over a rock, and when he looked up, his cousin Rachel was there to help him up.

   Alex said hi to his cousin.

_____

_____

_____

_____

Extra Practice: Try connecting the following two unrelated sentences with a transition phrase or sentence.

   Alison heaved her book-filled bag onto her shoulder and went into the library.

   Alison scrambled around on the floor searching for her favorite pen.

_____

_____

_____

_____

_____

© Macmillan/McGraw-Hill

You can change a base word that is a verb to a noun by adding *-ion* or *-ation* to the word's ending. For example, to change the verb **navigate** to a noun, drop the last **e** and add *-ion*: **navigation**.

Sometimes, because of the way the word sounds, you have to use the alternative ending *-ation*, as in **commendation**.

A good test for which ending to use would be to see if you can pronounce the word with the *-ion* ending. **Commendion** is very hard to say, so we use the *-ation* ending for **commendation**.

A. Read each verb below and decide which ending you should use to change it to a noun. Try out the *-ion* ending first. If that does not sound correct, then use *-ation*. Write your nouns on the lines that follow each base word.

1. consider _____   5. confess _____

2. decorate _____   6. discuss _____

3. promote _____   7. confuse _____

4. act _____   8. express _____

B. Use four of the nouns in sentences of your own.

9. _____

_____

10. _____

_____

11. _____

_____

12. _____

_____

© Macmillan/McGraw-Hill

 R 1.0 Word Analysis, Fluency, and Systematic Vocabulary Development

A. Match each vocabulary word to its synonym.

dilapidated	decades	rafters	instinctively
swiveled	auction	decrease	shakily

1. unsteadily _____

2. decayed _____

3. lower _____

4. naturally _____

5. turned _____

6. tens _____

7. sale _____

8. beams _____

B. Write sentences using four of the vocabulary words.

9. _____

_____

10. _____

_____

11. _____

_____

12. _____

_____

Read the paragraphs below. Describe both sides of each argument. Then give an explanation for your judgment.

In the nineteenth century, many museums increased the sizes of their collections. They bought valuable objects for very low prices and carried them far from their places of origin. The British Museum bought works of art in Greece and Egypt and brought them back to London. Museums in the United States acquired many Native American objects. Some people say that these objects should be returned to their original owners. Others say that these objects should remain in museums for people everywhere to enjoy.

1. First argument: _____

   _____

2. Second argument: _____

   _____

3. Your judgment: _____

   _____

Some people want to stop companies that make certain products from advertising. They believe that advertising some products, such as chewing tobacco, encourages young ball players to begin bad habits. Other people deny that advertising has much influence. Some also believe that companies should have the right to advertise. They believe that advertising is a form of free speech, and free speech should be protected.

4. First argument: _____

   _____

5. Second argument: _____

   _____

6. Your judgment: _____

   _____

© Macmillan/McGraw-Hill

CA R 2.0 Reading Comprehension (Focus on Informational Materials)

Name _____

As you read *Honus and Me*, fill in the Make Judgments Chart.

Action	Judgment

How does the information you wrote in this Make Judgments Chart help
you better understand *Honus and Me*?

As I read, I will pay attention to expression.

12	"Whoever wants to know the heart and mind of America had better learn baseball."
14	A famous historian wrote those words in the 1950s, when baseball had
25	been America's favorite sport for almost 100 years. People played it in
36	small towns all across the country. In the 1870s, many people lived in small
49	towns. Most worked on farms. Baseball was the perfect pastime for them.
61	Baseball was a rural game. It slowly became a favorite American sport.
73	People loved baseball for many reasons. Until the last 30 or 40
83	years, mostly boys had played sports. And most American boys grew up
94	playing baseball. They played it all summer long. They played in
105	schoolyards, on farm fields, and in parks. Wherever you could put out
117	four bases, you were likely to find kids playing baseball.
127	The first professional game of paid players took place in 1869 in
138	Cincinnati, Ohio. In 1876, the National League was formed. At the time,
149	no other organized sports were played. Professional baseball just made
159	sense to people. It had clear rules. And people enjoyed different things
171	in the game. Some loved memorizing the statistics of individual
181	players. Others admired favorite pitchers or hitters. Still others cheered
191	for their hometown teams. For many years, baseball was the most
202	popular sport in America. It was called America's pastime. 211

Comprehension Check

1. What is the author's purpose for writing this passage? **Author's Purpose**

2. Why would someone make a judgment about Americans based on baseball? **Make Judgments**

	Words Read	–	Number of Errors	=	Words Correct Score
First Read		–		=	
Second Read		–		=	

 R 1.1 Read aloud narrative and expository text fluently and accurately and with appropriate pacing, intonation, and **expression**.

Name _____

Articles in magazines, newspapers, and textbooks are often accompanied by illustrations. **Photos** and illustrations enrich an article by showing the reader something words cannot. Often an illustration or a photo is accompanied by a **caption**, a sentence or two that describe what is in the picture. The caption gives the reader additional information.

Study the illustration and caption below. Use them to answer the questions.

Milwaukee, 1957, National League President Warren Giles presents Hank Aaron with the 1957 National League Most Valuable Player Award.

Henry "Hank" Aaron hit 755 home runs over his career. Not only did he break Babe Ruth's record for home runs—he also established 12 other major league career records. He averaged 33 home runs a year. He drove in more than 100 runs 15 times, including a record 13 seasons in a row.

1. Who is shown in the illustration? _____

2. What made Hank Aaron famous? _____

_____

3. How many home runs did Hank Aaron hit in his career? _____

_____

4. Where and when was the picture taken? _____

5. What award did Hank Aaron receive in 1957? _____

_____

 R 2.1 Identify the structural features of popular media (e.g., newspapers, magazines, online information) and use the features to obtain information.

A **thesaurus** lists a word's **antonyms**. Antonyms are words with opposite or nearly opposite meanings. In a thesaurus, the antonym is often the last part of the entry. It is usually marked *ant.*

Example: *decrease*: lower, reduce, subtract; *ant.* increase

The antonym, or the word with the opposite meaning, of *decrease* is *increase*.

A. Write the antonyms of the following words. Use a thesaurus if you need to.

1. movement: _____

2. problem: _____

3. collect: _____

4. many: _____

5. expensive: _____

6. depart: _____

7. shaky: _____

8. decayed: _____

B. Choose four of the words listed above and use them in sentences.

9. _____

_____

10. _____

_____

11. _____

_____

12. _____

_____

CA R 1.0 Word Analysis, Fluency, and Systematic Vocabulary Development

Name _____

Using the Word Study Steps

1. LOOK at the word.
2. SAY the word aloud.
3. STUDY the letters in the word.

4. WRITE the word.
5. CHECK the word.
   Did you spell the word right?
   If not, go back to step 1.

A. Find the Words

Find and circle the spelling words hidden in each set of letters. Then write them on the line provided.

1. r e a c o n n e c t i o b s e r v a
2. t a t i o i n s p i l l u s t r a t e
3. c o n n c o n s u l t a t i n g s a
4. h e s i t a t i o n a t i o n a t s
5. r e p r e a c t i o b s e r v a t i
6. c o u s i n s t r u c t i o n r s a
7. b e s a s e p s e p a r a t i o n
8. r e p r e s e n t a c t i o n e r e
9. n i o t a r o b s e r v a t i o n
10. j u b a n i j i m i n s p i r e

Handwritten answers:
Reaconnect — iobserva
tation — spill — ust — rate
hesitation — at — ionats
repreacti — observation

_____
_____
_____
_____
_____
_____

B. Make a Puzzle

Make up a puzzle of your own using the space on this page. Give it to someone else to solve. Be sure to include at least five spelling words in your puzzle.

LC 1.5 Spell frequently misspelled words correctly
(e.g., *their, they're, there*).

Honus and Me • Grade 6/Unit 3   187

Name _____

A. Proofreading Activity

There are five spelling mistakes in the paragraph below. Circle the misspelled words. Write the words correctly on the lines below.

Solving a mystery is often a difficult task. However, with a thorough investigation and careful observattion you may be able to solve the case. First you must seperate fact from fiction, by determining what you know to be true or false. It may be necessary to consolt with experts to determine how best to go about solving your mystery. They may be able to offer a conection, based on the information you collected, that you may not have noticed at first. Following their instrucsion may make it easier for you to solve your case.

1. _____   2. _____   3. _____

4. _____   5. _____

B. Writing Activity

Write a set of instructions for a task you know how to do well. Then trade papers with a partner to check if your instructions are clear to them. Use five spelling words.

_____

_____

_____

_____

_____

_____

_____

_____

LC 1.5 Spell frequently misspelled words correctly (e.g., *their, they're, there*).

- Some **irregular verbs** have special spellings when used with the helping verbs **have**, **has**, or **had**.

Present	Past	Past (with *have*, *has*, *had*)
think	thought	thought
tear	tore	torn
sink	sank	sunk
catch	caught	caught
freeze	froze	frozen
break	broke	broken
blow	blew	blown
teach	taught	taught
wear	wore	worn
know	knew	known
drink	drank	drunk
choose	chose	chosen
speak	spoke	spoken

**Each sentence contains an incorrect form of an irregular verb.
Write the correct verb form on the line provided.**

1. As soon as Sarah stepped out onto the stage, she freezed.

   She froze

2. Albert finally finded the prop he needed for Act Two. _find_

3. Sarah had speaked with the director about her lines in Act One.

   spoke

4. She thinked that the speech was too long. _thinks_

5. But the director had choosed Sarah for a reason; he knew she could do it.

   chosed

The writer of this play's dialogue did not proofread for mistakes. Rewrite the dialogue, correcting any mistakes made in punctuation. Make sure verb forms are used correctly.

Scene 1

LaWonda on stage at rehearsal. With her is Danny and Sarah.

LaWonda loudly "Danny, you keep standed in front of Sarah! You're supposing to be behind her.

Danny defiantly "Who making you boss?"

LaWonda gesturing with the script "See? It sayed so right here!"

Sarah looked at her script, then pointing backstage "She's right, Danny. You belonged back there."

Danny sighing, then walking backstage "Two against one. Okay."

_____

_____

_____

_____

_____

_____

_____

_____

_____

_____

_____

_____

_____

© Macmillan/McGraw-Hill

1. Read the following passages:

Passage 1:

Jessica heard the buzzing of the alarm. Instantly, she ran to the window to check outside to see if the weatherman was right. Snow! At least a foot of it! Cars drove by, slipping and sliding. Trees bent with the weight of the snow. There would definitely be no school today. Quickly, Jessica jumped back in bed and covered herself up, giggling.

Passage 2:

Will ignored the alarm when it went off. He knew from checking the Web that there would be no school today, and listening, he heard wind gusts and icy snowflakes pelting. He smiled a drowsy smile and buried his head under the pillows.

2. List 3 ways in which the students' reactions are similar:

    a.

    b.

    c.

3. Now, pretend you are writing an essay in which you are comparing the students' reactions. Write a transition between the two passages that emphasizes how they are similar.

_____

_____

_____

_____

_____

_____

_____

_____

The suffix *-ion* means an action or a condition. When you add
it to the end of a verb, it changes the verb to a noun, as in **act +
ion = action**. Sometimes you drop an **e** from the end of the base
word when you add the ending, as in **create + ion = creation**.
Sometimes you have to change the spelling at the end of the base
word to make the new word easier to say.

Examples:

The last letters **d** or **de** become an **s**.   *explode + ion = explosion*
The last letter **t** becomes **ss**.   *permit + ion = permission*
The last letters **eive** become **ept**.   *receive + ion = reception*

**A. Add the *-ion* suffix to each word. Make the necessary spelling
changes.**

1. extend _____

2. implode _____

3. perceive _____

4. pretend _____

5. transmit _____

6. corrode _____

7. divide _____

8. emit _____

9. deceive _____

10. transmit _____

**B. Choose two of the words you made and use each in a sentence of
your own. Underline the *-ion* words you use.**

11. _____

12. _____

© Macmillan/McGraw-Hill

 R 1.0 Word Analysis, Fluency, and Systematic Vocabulary Development

Name _____

A. Write the vocabulary word that best matches each clue.

summit	awesome	specialists	deteriorated
maturity	guidance	peripheral	typical

1. This is what you need when you are lost. _____

2. This is what you show when you act like a grown-up. _____

3. These kinds of doctors work only in one area of medicine; neurosurgeons

    are examples of _____.

4. You might use this word to describe something that causes wonder.

    _____

5. If you reach the top of the mountain, you are standing on this.

    _____

6. You might use this word to describe something ordinary.

    _____

7. You use this kind of vision to see things out of the corner of your eye.

    _____

8. If something has gotten worse, it has done this. _____

B. Write two sentences using four vocabulary words from above. Underline the words you use.

9. _____

    _____

10. _____

    _____

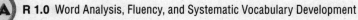

> An informational text contains facts about a particular topic. It usually also reveals the author's position, or **perspective**, on that topic. Words such as *best, worst, should,* and *must* express opinions and signal the reader that the author is expressing her or his perspective.

Read the passage and answer the questions that follow.

The Paralympic Games are great because they offer athletes with a disability the chance to compete on a world stage. In 1948, a sports competition was held for World War II veterans with spinal cord injuries. In 1960, after the Olympics in Rome, the first official Paralympic Summer Games took place. The first Paralympic Winter Games were played in 1976, and in that year, the competition was opened to athletes with disabilities other than spinal cord injuries. Today, athletes who are visually impaired or blind, have amputated limbs, spinal cord injuries, or motor impairment due to stroke, brain injury, or cerebral palsy can enter the Paralympics. Furthermore, athletes are grouped by ability, not by medical classification.

1. Does the author of this passage have a strongly expressed point of view about the Paralympic Games? _____

2. Can you infer anything about the author's perspective from the information provided? _____

_____

3. What word from the passage signals that the author is expressing an opinion. _____

4. What type of information could the author add to the passage to express a clearer perspective on the Paralympic Games?

_____

_____

_____

© Macmillan/McGraw-Hill

 R 2.0 Reading Comprehension (Focus on Informational Materials)

As you read *Seeing Things His Own Way*, fill in the Author's Perspective Chart.

Author's Perspective Chart

Clues	Author's Perspective

How does the information you wrote on this Author's Perspective Chart help you better understand *Seeing Things His Own Way*?

Name _____

As I read, I will pay attention to intonation and phrasing.

	Marla Runyan is a competitive Olympic athlete. She is
9	also legally blind. Though you might guess that Marla is
19	very different from other athletes, in most ways, she really
29	isn't. She has had injuries and disappointments. She has had
39	victories, too. She has changed coaches and tried new events.
49	She has been good at a lot of things, and **awesome** at a few.
63	She is stubborn, competitive, and proud.
69	What does make Marla different is that she lacks full
79	vision. She has only **peripheral** vision. This means she can
89	see only the outer edges of what most people normally view.
100	For example, if she looks at a picture of a person, she
112	might see only the top of his head, his fingertips, and his
124	shoes. The rest of his body is a blur of colors.
135	Marla's vision problems are uncommon in the world of
144	top-notch athletes, but what really makes her different is that
154	she hasn't let poor vision stop her from doing what she loves
166	and doing her best. 170

Comprehension Check

1. How would you summarize Marla's athletic career? **Summarize**

2. What does the author want you to know about Marla? **Author's Purpose**

	Words Read	–	Number of Errors	=	Words Correct Score
First Read		–		=	
Second Read		–		=	

 R 1.1 Read aloud narrative and expository text fluently and accurately and with appropriate pacing, **intonation**, and expression.

Name _____

Diagrams are visual illustrations that show you how something is put together or arranged. When you look at a diagram, make sure you read all the **labels** so you can be clear about what is presented. Tables are used to organize information to make it easily accessible.

Use the diagram to answer the questions.

Bat Anatomy

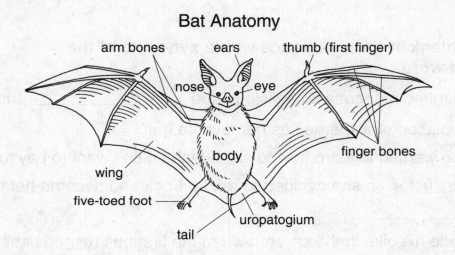

1. What does the diagram show? _____

2. What is the uropatagium? _____

_____

3. Where are a bat's thumbs located? _____

4. How many fingers do bats have? _____

5. How many toes do bats have? _____

6. Use the lines below to write a paragraph about bats. Use what you already knew about bats and what you might have learned from the diagram.

_____

_____

_____

R 2.1 Identify the structural features of popular media (e.g., newspapers, magazines, online information) and use the features to obtain information.

When you encounter an unfamiliar word, check the context within which it is used. One kind of context clue is a **synonym** of the word used in the same passage, often within the same sentence.

Example: The biker relied on her <u>peripheral</u>, or <u>side</u>, vision as she changed lanes.
The words **peripheral** and **side** are synonyms.

Fill in the blank in each sentence with a synonym of the underlined word.

1. Rachel found mangoes so <u>delicious</u> and _____ that they have replaced strawberries as her favorite fruit.

2. Madison wanted to learn how to ski, but she didn't want to pay for a ski <u>instructor</u>, so she decided to read a book and become her own _____.

3. José rode his bike in the city, but when the first bus <u>rushed</u> past him and then another car _____ by him, he decided city cycling wasn't for him.

4. Stephanie had an <u>itinerary</u> of all the places to visit in Spain, but she lost her travel _____ somewhere along the way.

5. When Alejandro heard the glass inside the box <u>break</u> and _____, he knew his mom's present would have to be replaced.

6. Before he <u>departs</u> for work, Mitchell turns off all the lights in his home and then he _____.

7. Katrina knew the stone was <u>artificial</u>, but she thought the _____ diamond looked very real.

8. Despite looking confident, inside Raja was <u>anxious</u> and _____.

© Macmillan/McGraw-Hill

 R 1.0 Word Analysis, Fluency, and Systematic Vocabulary Development

Name _____

Using the Word Study Steps

1. LOOK at the word.

2. SAY the word aloud.

3. STUDY the letters in the word.

4. WRITE the word.

5. CHECK the word.
   Did you spell the word right?
   If not, go back to step 1.

Missing Letters

Fill in the missing letters to form spelling words.

1. explos _____

2. explan _____

3. _____ laim

4. decis _____

5. exclam _____

6. collis _____

7. _____ cide

8. _____ lode

9. permis _____

10. inclus _____

11. _____ lide

12. admis _____

13. omis _____ .

14. _____ lude

15. divis _____

© Macmillan/McGraw-Hill

LC 1.5 Spell frequently misspelled words correctly
(e.g., *their, they're, there*).

Seeing Things His Own Way
Grade 6/Unit 4

199

A. Proofreading Activity

There are five spelling mistakes in the paragraph below. Circle the misspelled words. Write the words correctly on the lines below.

After watching a documentary on rock climbers, Raphael made a decition that he would like to try it. He read a book on the subject that gave a clear explanasion of how to train. He asked the coach at his school to inclued him in the school's training team. After several months of training, Raphael felt confident enough to ask his coach for permision to try out for the rock-climbing team at the local gym. His coach agreed, and Raphael was so happy after the tryouts to learn that the gym would addmit him to the rock-climbing competition. For Raphael, his dedication to making the competition was more impressive and rewarding than whether or not he won.

1. _____   2. _____   3. _____

4. _____   5. _____

B. Writing Activity

Have you ever worked really hard to try to achieve a specific goal? Write a short paragraph about a goal that required determination to achieve. Use five spelling words.

_____

_____

_____

_____

_____

_____

_____

_____

© Macmillan/McGraw-Hill

 LC 1.5 Spell frequently misspelled words correctly (e.g., *their, they're, there*).

Name _____

- Singular pronouns are *I, you, he, she, it, me, him,* and *her*.
- Plural pronouns are *we, you, they, us,* and *them*.

Fill in the blank with an appropriate pronoun. Write an *S* if the pronoun is singular. Write a *P* if the pronoun is plural.

1. _____ wonder if Peter will come hiking. _____

2. After breakfast, _____ went on a hike. _____

3. The hikers take plenty of water with _____.

    _____

4. Will Peter and Susanna hike with _____? _____

5. Spanish is an interesting language, and _____ is easy to

    learn. _____

6. _____ is interested in studying Spanish. _____

7. Peter signed up for a language class, and then _____ bought

    the books for it. _____

8. The language school was far away, but Peter enjoyed walking to

    _____. _____

9. Peter and Susanna both studied Spanish, and then _____

    studied French. _____

10. Peter called Susanna and asked _____ to lunch.

    _____

Name _____

- A **pronoun** is a word that takes the place of one or more nouns.
- The **antecedent** or **referent** of a pronoun is the word or group of words to which the pronoun refers. Pronouns and antecedents must agree.

Underline any pronouns that do not agree with their antecedents. Then rewrite the interview, using the correct singular and plural pronouns, capitalization, and punctuation.

REPORTER: Today my special guest is Brian Plomaco, the famed one-armed mountaineer from Utah. Brian, how did him get your start in mountain climbing?

PLOMACO: He's glad I asked. Him began climbing mountains with my father when it was only five years old.

REPORTER: She must have been a very energetic child!

PLOMACO: Yes, we was.

REPORTER: What is the highest mountain they have climbed?

PLOMACO: Him climbed K2 last summer. That is the climb you am most proud of.

_____

_____

_____

_____

_____

_____

_____

_____

_____

_____

 LC 1.0 Written and Oral English Language Conventions

Name _____

1. Read the sentences below. Choose one sentence. First fill in the blank. Then use evidence to prove it.

   Roller coasters are _____.

   Walking is _____.

2. Here is an example for you:

   Assertion: Roller coasters are **exciting**.

Evidence: *People scream*.
**   *Roller coasters rocket around curves*.**
**   *People get flipped upside down*.**

Roller coasters are exciting. I saw people screaming as the roller coaster rocketed around the curve and flipped upside down.

The evidence in this example proves that the assertion (Roller coasters are exciting.) is true. Notice that the more strong verbs and details that you use, the more convincing you will be.

3. _____ are/is _____.

Evidence: _____

_____

_____

Sometimes the vowel sounds of base words change with the addition of suffixes. A long sound might become a short sound. For example, *wise* has a long *i* sound, but *wisdom* has a short *i* sound.

A. Read the words. Explain how the underlined vowel sound in the first word changes with the addition of a suffix. Underline the changed vowel in the second word.

1. pron<u>ou</u>nce   pronunciation _____

_____

_____

2. hum<u>a</u>n   humanity _____

_____

3. s<u>ou</u>th   southern _____

_____

4. adm<u>i</u>re   admiration _____

_____

5. cr<u>i</u>me   criminal _____

_____

B. Choose three of the words listed above and use them in sentences. Use at least one of the words in each sentence.

6. _____

_____

7. _____

_____

8. _____

_____

CA **R 1.0** Word Analysis, Fluency, and Systematic Vocabulary Development

Name _____

A. Write each vocabulary word next to its definition.

demonstration	prominent	luxury	adept
spectators	prevail	maneuvered	collective

1. involving all members of a group _____

2. people who watch _____

3. triumph _____

4. widely known or famous _____

5. highly skilled _____

6. showing the value of a product _____

7. changed direction and position for a purpose _____

8. condition of having comfort and pleasure _____

B. Choose four of the vocabulary words and write a sentence for each.

9. _____

_____

10. _____

_____

11. _____

_____

12. _____

_____

Facts are statements that can be proven true. **Opinions** are statements than cannot be proven true.

Each statement below is either a fact or an opinion. If the statement is a fact, write *fact* on the line provided. If the statement is an opinion, write *opinion* on the line provided.

1. Bicycling is one of many forms of exercise that young people can do.

    _____

2. Mountain bikes should be used only in the mountains, not on city streets.

    _____

3. Bicycles are a form of transportation in many parts of the world.

    _____

4. Bicycles are better than cars because they produce less pollution.

    _____

5. Learning to ride a bicycle is the easiest experience you will ever have.

    _____

6. To reduce the use of fossil fuels, people could use bicycles as their main

    form of transportation. _____

7. Bicyclists must follow the law when riding on city streets.

    _____

8. Bicycles are the best way to travel. _____

9. You don't need to worry about wearing a bicycle helmet if you're not riding

    in the street. _____

10. Before you ride a bicycle, you should always check to make sure the

    brakes are working properly. _____

© Macmillan/McGraw-Hill

 R 2.0 Reading Comprehension (Focus on Informational Materials)

Name _____

As you read *Major Taylor*, fill in the Fact and Opinion Chart.

Fact	Opinion

How does the information you wrote in this Fact and Opinion Chart help
you better understand *Major Taylor*?

As I read, I will pay attention to pacing.

	Did you know that the first bicycles were for sport and pleasure?
12	Some of the earliest bikes were luxury toys for the rich. Today, people
25	ride bikes for many different reasons. Children ride bikes for fun.
36	Your mom or dad may ride to work or to the store. Some people, such
51	as bicycle messengers, even use bikes to do their job.
61	The professional cyclist made the sport of cycling popular.
70	These athletes spend their time training and competing in national
80	and international cycling events. They appear on television. They are
90	front-page news in newspapers. Some have become the new athletes
100	of the year in sports magazines.
106	But there is one professional cyclist who changed cycling history.
116	He is Lance Armstrong. He won the Tour de France six times. The Tour
130	de France is the greatest race in cycling. No one has ever won this race
145	so many times. But there's more. In the midst of his cycling career,
158	Lance had to overcome cancer. As a cancer survivor, Mr. Armstrong
169	made the greatest comeback in cycling history.
176	Most of Lance's racing bikes are sleek and incredibly lightweight.
186	This is quite a dramatic change from early bicycles. 195

Comprehension Check

1. What is the author's purpose for including Lance Armstrong in this passage? **Author's Purpose**

2. How do you think the changes from the early bicycles helped Lance Armstrong win the Tour de France six times? **Draw Conclusions**

© Macmillan/McGraw-Hill

	Words Read	–	Number of Errors	=	Words Correct Score
First Read		–		=	
Second Read		–		=	

 R 1.1 Read aloud narrative and expository text fluently and accurately and with appropriate **pacing**, intonation, and expression.

Name _____

Poetry uses words in special ways.

Assonance is the repetition of the same middle vowel sound in two or more closely grouped words. Example: *pudgy bug*

Onomatopoeia is the use of a word to sound like or imitate what it describes. Examples: *chirp, bleep, bang*

My pup and I take to the trail,
Up and down the hills we sail,
On paws, on bike, together we race,
My metal gears click into place.
Thump, bump, my tires pound,
Pant, pant, my partner's sound.
Every time by just a whisker,
The dog wins, he's just brisker.
Woof, woof, he barks in victory,
That's enough, I say in misery.
I'm positive I've seen him wink.
I haven't got a chance, I think.

1. Which words have assonance? _____

_____

2. Which words show onomatopoeia? _____

_____

3. How does the author use humor to show how he feels about his pet?

_____

_____

4. Write two more lines for this poem that have either assonance or show

onomatopoeia. _____

_____

© Macmillan/McGraw-Hill

Using **analogies** requires you to identify the relationships between words. Sometimes analogies can be synonyms or antonyms. Other times, one word might be a category of another or might be something the other does. Analogies are written like this:

diners : eat :: spectators : _____

Read the analogy like this: Diners are to eat as spectators are to _____.

Your job is to fill in the blank. First you must identify the relationship between *diners* and *eat*. When you realize that *eat* is something a *diner* does, you should then think about what a *spectator* does. This will give you the answer, *watch*.

Circle the letter of the word that best completes each analogy.

1. reader : book :: rider :
   a. magazine
   b. supper
   c. bicycle
   d. art

2. biology : science :: geometry :
   a. numbers
   b. Math
   c. shapes
   d. algebra

3. car : steering wheel :: bike :
   a. wheels
   b. gears
   c. brakes
   d. handlebars

4. automobile : motor :: novel :
   a. plot
   b. book
   c. poem
   d. author

© Macmillan/McGraw-Hill

 R 1.0 Word Analysis, Fluency, and Systematic Vocabulary Development

Name _____

Using the Word Study Steps

1. LOOK at the word.

2. SAY the word aloud.

3. STUDY the letters in the word.

4. WRITE the word.

5. CHECK the word.
   Did you spell the word right?
   If not, go back to step 1.

Find Rhyming Words

Circle the word in each row that rhymes with the spelling word on the left.

1. **metal**	settle	retail	hospital
2. **refer**	suffer	occur	after
3. **reside**	cupid	rustle	divide
4. **competition**	completion	position	missile
5. **national**	notional	emotional	rational
6. **momentous**	momentum	clearance	apprentice
7. **ignition**	function	caution	musician
8. **compete**	discrete	abrupt	create
9. **crime**	team	rhyme	lemon
10. **reference**	deference	prance	clearance
11. **finality**	jollity	morality	frailty
12. **nation**	station	mission	suction
13. **ignite**	delight	crate	align
14. **final**	regal	little	vinyl
15. **original**	petal	cable	aboriginal

© Macmillan/McGraw-Hill

LC 1.5 Spell frequently misspelled words correctly
(e.g., *their, they're, there*).

Practice

A. Proofreading Activity

There are five spelling mistakes in the paragraph below. Circle the misspelled words. Write the words correctly on the lines below.

Today was a truly momentis occasion in my life. I was so happy because I won a qualifying race of the nasional bike tournament for children. The compitition was eight miles long. We raced through the streets of the neighborhood in which I rezide. During the finle mile I knew I was winning because there was nobody racing near me. I was so proud when I won.

1. _____   2. _____   3. _____

4. _____   5. _____

B. Writing Activity

What's one accomplishment that you are very proud of? Write a diary entry about your accomplishment and what made it special. Use five spelling words.

_____

_____

_____

_____

_____

_____

_____

_____

 LC 1.5 Spell frequently misspelled words correctly (e.g., *their, they're, there*).

Name _____

- An **object pronoun** is used as the object of a verb or as the object of a preposition, such as *for*, *at*, *with*, or *to*. Use an object pronoun when the pronoun is part of a compound object.
- *Me*, *you*, *him*, *her*, *it*, *us*, and *them* are object pronouns.
- An **indefinite pronoun** does not refer to a specific person or thing.
- *Anyone*, *someone*, *nobody*, *both*, *several* and *all* are indefinite pronouns.

A. Put brackets [ ] around each incorrect object pronoun. Write the correct object pronoun on the line.

1. Janis tried not to laugh at I. _____

2. The diving teacher handed the flippers to she. _____

3. Raul said, "Please bring these flippers to they." _____

4. Will Janis come into the water with Raul and I? _____

5. Between you and I, scuba diving is a little scary. _____

6. I finally learned how to dive, and it brought I great happiness.

   _____

B. Put brackets around the indefinite pronoun in parentheses that correctly completes each sentence.

7. The teacher asked if (us, anyone) wanted to jump in the water.

8. At first (nobody, her) said anything.

9. Suddenly (them, several) raised their hands.

10. Before the teacher could speak, (me, all) were in the water.

© Macmillan/McGraw-Hill

- A **subject pronoun** is used as the subject of a sentence. Use a subject pronoun when the pronoun is part of a compound subject. *I, you, he, she, it, we,* and *they* are subject pronouns.
- An **object pronoun** is used as the object of a verb or as the object of a preposition, such as *for, at, with,* or *to.* Use an object pronoun when the pronoun is part of a compound object. *Me, you, him, her, it, us,* and *them* are object pronouns.

Proofread and rewrite the scientific observation using the correct subject and object pronouns. Correct capitalization and punctuation.

    This was my first time scuba diving. i took several weeks of classes at the YMCA to get certified. I and my instructor spent hours in the pool, and i was excited as i strapped on my gear and tipped into the water. The first animal me saw was a moray eel! Me had been warned about eels, which like to stay in shallow water and hide under rocks. Him was beautifully colored and at least three feet long. me and my instructor truly enjoyed seeing this incredible animal up close.

_____

_____

_____

_____

_____

_____

© Macmillan/McGraw-Hill

 LC 1.0 Written and Oral English Language Conventions

1. Many times, using a speaker's actual words makes an assertion more powerful.

2. Read these two sentences:

   Haley loves to play basketball.

   Wilson is afraid of heights.

3. Read these examples that show how you could have Haley say something that makes the assertion more convincing.

   "I sleep with my head on a basketball and wake up with little basketball dimples on my cheeks," Haley told her friends before practice.

   "I wish I could play basketball every day," Haley announced at dinner.

   "I want to play on a professional woman's basketball league," Haley told her coach.

4. Choose one of the sentences above. Change that sentence so that you use a quote to show what the narrator is saying (asserting). Punctuate carefully.

   _____

   _____

   _____

   _____

   _____

   _____

   _____

   _____

   _____

   _____

   _____

Words can include a **prefix** at the beginning, a base word, and a **suffix** at the end. Knowing the meanings of some common prefixes and suffixes, along with meanings of base words, can help you figure out the meaning of a new word.

Prefix	Meaning	Suffix	Meaning
un-, dis-	not	*-ful*	full of
out-	in a way that is greater	*-ment*	result of or state of
en-	put in or on, or cover with	*-ly*	in the manner of
re-	again or back	*-ness*	a state or condition of

A. In the words below, circle the prefix and underline the suffix.
Then write the meaning of the word on the line following it.

1. unkindness _____

2. enclose _____

3. rearrangement _____

4. unthankful _____

5. outgrow _____

6. disagreement _____

7. retirement _____

8. unhappiness _____

9. disentangle _____

10. unpleasantness _____

B. Choose two of the words above and use each in a sentence of
your own.

11. _____

_____

12. _____

_____

Name _____

Use the clues to complete the crossword.

inspiration   extremely   revealed
attended   managed

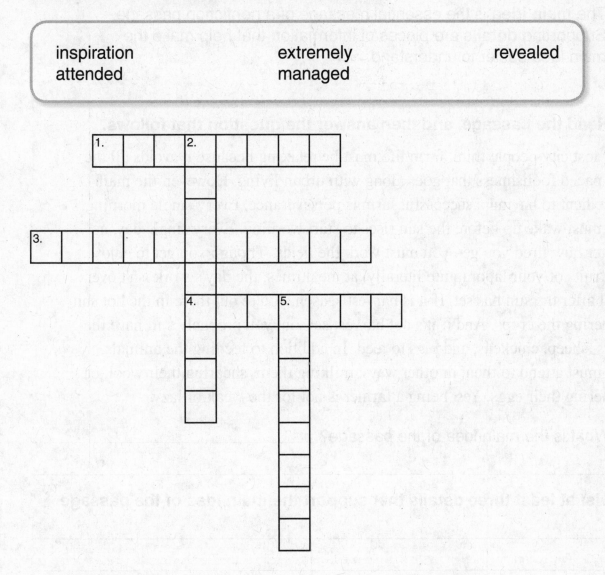

Across

1. made known
3. something that causes you to think creatively
4. was able to do something difficult

Down

2. way beyond normal
5. went to an event

R 1.0 Word Analysis, Fluency, and Systematic Vocabulary Development.

Take a Bow • Grade 6/Unit 4   **217**

© Macmillan/McGraw-Hill

> The **main idea** is the essential message of a nonfiction passage.
> Supporting **details** are pieces of information that help make the
> main idea easier to understand.

A. Read the passage, and then answer the question that follows.

Most city people think farm life must be relaxing because it avoids all the
fast-paced foolishness that goes along with urban living. However, the main
ingredient to having a successful farm is perseverance. Every single morning,
you must wake up before the sun rises to start working. Every single day, no
matter how tired you get, you must work the fields. Though you get to enjoy
the fruits of your labor (quite literally) at mealtimes, the day's work isn't over
until after the sun has set. If it is harvest season, you're out there in the hot sun
gathering the crops. And if it's not harvest season, you probably still have the
cows, sheep, chickens, and pigs to feed. In addition to feeding the animals,
you must attend to them in other ways: milking them, shearing their wool, or
gathering their eggs. Yes, being a farmer is not for the weak or lazy.

1. What is the main idea of the passage? _____

_____

B. List at least three details that support the main idea of the passage.

2. _____

3. _____

4. _____

© Macmillan/McGraw-Hill

R 2.3 Connect and clarify main ideas by identifying their relationships
to other sources and related topics.

As you read *Take a Bow*, fill in the Main Idea and Details Chart.

Main Idea _____

_____

Detail 1 _____

_____

Detail 2 _____

_____

↓

Summary _____

_____

_____

How does the information you wrote in the Main Idea and Details Chart
help you summarize *Take a Bow*?

R 2.3 Connect and clarify main ideas by identifying their relationships
to other sources and related topics.

As I read, I will pay attention to my phrasing.

	The Midwest floods hit Iowa in July, 1993. On July 10, heavy
10	rains poured down on ground that was already soaked. The
20	next day, the rising Raccoon River flooded. River waters broke
30	through the levee protecting Iowa's capital city of Des Moines.
40	A levee is a man-made wall. Levees keep river waters from
51	flooding populated areas. But sometimes they fail.
58	The raging waters flooded Des Moines' water-treatment plant.
66	The plant shut down. For 12 days, 250,000 people in
75	Des Moines were without clean water for drinking. Residents
84	couldn't bathe, wash their clothes, or even flush their toilets.
94	There wasn't enough water to use in fighting fires. The mayor
105	of Des Moines shut down all but the most essential businesses.
116	Des Moines needed clean water—and fast. Soon help was there.
127	Help came from the Federal Emergency Management Agency,
134	or FEMA. FEMA goes in to help when the President of the
145	United States declares a place a disaster area. The agency tries
157	to mitigate, or help make better, some of the problems. It finds
169	people shelter. It repairs buildings and provides insurance
178	money. In Des Moines, FEMA took charge of getting fresh
188	water to the city. 192

Comprehension Check

1. Why is flooding a problem? **Make Generalizations**

2. How did FEMA help Des Moines? **Main Idea and Details**

	Words Read	–	Number of Errors	=	Words Correct Score
First Read		–		=	
Second Read		–		=	

© Macmillan/McGraw-Hill

 R 1.1 Read aloud narrative and expository text fluently and accurately and with appropriate pacing, intonation, and expression.

When you need to research a topic, you can use a search engine to explore the **Internet**. You will need to think of key words to enter into the search box. Enter the words, click on *search*, and the search engine will find a list of Web sites. Each Web site listing will have a brief description and a Web address. Click on an underlined link to open a new Web page.

Best Web Browser | Hurricane Andrew | | Search |

1. <u>Tropical Storm Center</u> - **Hurricane Andrew**
   The Tropical Storm Center's main page on **Hurricane Andrew** of 1992
   http://www.tsc.gov
2. <u>National Weather Home Page</u> - **Hurricane Andrew**
   Hurricane Andrew a very destructive United States **hurricane**
   http://www.nationalweather.gov
3. <u>U.S. Satellite Pictures</u> - **Hurricane Andrew**
   Satellite pictures and upper-air data of **Hurricane Andrew**
   http://www.ussatellitepics.gov
4. <u>Aftermath Photos</u> - **Hurricane Andrew**
   Photographs of damage after Florida's worst hurricane
   http://www.andrewpics.com
5. <u>10 Years after **Hurricane Andrew**</u>: America's Newspaper
   People's lives 10 years after the destructive **Hurricane Andrew**
   http://www.americasnewspaper.com

Use the search results above to answer the questions.

1. Which key words were used to search for information? _____

2. Which sites might have information about the storm's origins?

_____

_____

3. Which national newspaper has an article on Andrew?

_____

4. If you needed pictures, which sites would likely be most helpful?

_____

5. If you wanted to search for the effects of Andrew on Miami, which keywords

would you use? _____

R 2.1 Identify the structural features of popular media (e.g., newspapers, magazines, online information) and use the features to obtain information.

Name _____

Sequence Writing Frame

A. Summarize *Take a Bow*. Use the Sequence Writing Frame below.

Sarah Chang is a great violinist.

In 1980, Sarah Chang was born to _____
_____.

When she was three, _____
_____.

Two years later, _____
_____.

When she was nine, _____
_____.

By the time she reached her teens, _____
_____.

Today, Sarah Chang _____
_____.

B. Rewrite the completed summary on another sheet of paper. Keep it as a model for writing a summary of an article or selection using this text structure.

© Macmillan/McGraw-Hill

The meaning of an unfamiliar word can often be determined by understanding the surrounding words in the sentence or paragraph. Using **context clues**, or hints from the surrounding words, to determine the meaning of unfamiliar words is an important skill.

Read each sentence and look at the underlined word. Use context clues to determine the meaning of the word, and write the definition on the line provided. Then use the word in a sentence of your own.

1. His <u>absence</u> was noticed by everyone immediately; the class couldn't put on the play without the lead actor.

   Definition: _____

   Sentence: _____

   _____

2. I would like to <u>dedicate</u> this story to my grandmother, who inspired me to become a storyteller.

   Definition: _____

   Sentence: _____

   _____

3. The farmers were delighted to see that the crops were <u>plentiful</u> this year.

   Definition: _____

   Sentence: _____

   _____

4. She knew the <u>honorable</u> thing to do would be to tell her mother about the incident, but she just couldn't bring herself to do it.

   Definition: _____

   Sentence: _____

   _____

R 1.4 Monitor expository text for unknown words or words with novel meanings by using word, sentence, and paragraph clues to determine meaning.

Name _____

Using the Word Study Steps

1. LOOK at the word.

2. SAY the word aloud.

3. STUDY the letters in the word.

4. WRITE the word.

5. CHECK the word.
   Did you spell the word right?
   If not, go back to step 1.

Alphabetical Order

A. Write the spelling words in alphabetical order.

1. _____   11. _____

2. _____   12. _____

3. _____   13. _____

4. _____   14. _____

5. _____   15. _____

6. _____   16. _____

7. _____   17. _____

8. _____   18. _____

9. _____   19. _____

10. _____   20. _____

Write the Words

B. Use the lines below to practice writing the spelling words.

_____ _____ _____ _____

_____ _____ _____ _____

_____ _____ _____ _____

_____ _____ _____ _____

© Macmillan/McGraw-Hill

LC 1.5 Spell frequently misspelled words correctly
(e.g., *their, they're, there*).

Proofreading

A. There are five spelling mistakes in the paragraph below. Circle the misspelled words. Write the words correctly on the lines below.

Jude experienced great unhappyness when he failed his science exam. He failed because he answered most of the questions incorrectley. When his friends were discussing how well they had done on the exam, Jude felt like an outsidr. His teacher told him that he should not feel discoragment toward the class. His teacher felt that if Jude studied extra hard for the next exam he would be able to experience the injoyment of doing well in the class. Jude's teacher turned out to be correct. Jude studied hard and asked for extra help for the next exam and did very well.

1. _____   2. _____   3. _____

4. _____   5. _____

Writing Activity

B. Did you ever feel like you had to work twice as hard for something that came more easily to a friend? Write a story about the experience and what you learned from it. Use five spelling words.

_____

_____

_____

_____

_____

_____

_____

_____

_____

CA LC 1.5 Spell frequently misspelled words correctly
(e.g., *their, they're, there*).

Take a Bow • **Grade 6/Unit 4** 225

- Some **possessive pronouns** can stand alone: *mine, yours, his, hers, its, ours, yours, theirs.*
- Do not confuse the pronouns *its, your, their,* and *theirs* with the contractions *it's, you're, they're,* and *there's.*

A. Find the possessive pronoun in each of the following sentences. Write it on the line.

1. The patio chairs that blew into the neighbors' yard are not ours.

   _____

2. Mr. Sanchez looked at them, but they were not his. _____

3. The red bicycle, however, is mine. _____

4. The Laninghams finally identified the patio chairs as theirs.

   _____

5. Mrs. York said that the flower pot was hers. _____

B. Circle the pronoun in parentheses that correctly completes each sentence.

6. Is the bicycle (you'res, yours)?

7. (It's, Its) handlebars are totally rusted from the rain.

8. The car that the tree fell on is (theirs, there's).

9. (My, Mine) is the gray car in the driveway.

10. Two of (it's, its) tires are flat.

11. Is the battery pack (you'res, yours)?

12. I believe it is (theirs, there's).

LC 1.0 Written and Oral English Language Conventions

Name _____

- A **possessive pronoun** takes the place of a possessive noun. It shows who or what owns something.
- Some possessive pronouns are used before nouns and cannot stand alone: *my, you, his, her, its, our, your, their.*

Find errors in the use of possessive pronouns, contractions, punctuation, or capitalization in the fictional narrative below. Then rewrite the narrative correctly.

"How can I help?"

This was the only thought on young Pablo's mind after the hurricane as he looked at the fallen trees toppled power lines and homes without roofs in there town. "Is that bicycle you'res asked Mr. Sanchez.

Pablo said "Yes, its mine."

"Then jump on it's seat and ride to the community center. you can help make 10,000 ham and cheese sandwiches for folks who were evacuated.

_____

_____

_____

_____

_____

_____

_____

_____

_____

_____

Writing Rubric

	4 Excellent	3 Good	2 Fair	1 Unsatisfactory
	Ideas and Content/ Genre	Ideas and Content/ Genre	Ideas and Content/ Genre	Ideas and Content/ Genre
	Organization and Focus	Organization and Focus	Organization and Focus	Organization and Focus
	Sentence Structure/ Fluency	Sentence Structure/ Fluency	Sentence Structure/ Fluency	Sentence Structure/ Fluency
	Conventions	Conventions	Conventions	Conventions
	Word Choice	Word Choice	Word Choice	Word Choice
	Voice	Voice	Voice	Voice
	Presentation	Presentation	Presentation	Presentation

CA **W 1.0** Writing Strategies

Name _____

When you add the **prefixes** *co-*, *com-*, *con-*, *post-*, *pro-*, or *sub-* to words, you add a particular meaning to the word.

Here is a chart of some common prefixes and their meanings.

Prefix	co-, con-	post-	pro-	sub-
Meaning of Prefix	together or with	after	in front of or for	under
Example Word	contribute	postscript	promote	subway
Meaning of Word	give, as a group	written afterward	move forward	a route under ground

If you do not know the meaning of a word and you forget what the prefix means, think of another word that has the same prefix. This can help you understand new words.

Examples: contract, convert   postmark, postseason

Underline the Greek or Latin prefix in the following words. Then write the meaning of the complete word. Use a dictionary to help.

1. co-worker _____

2. committee _____

3. proportion _____

4. cooperate _____

5. profession _____

6. submit _____

7. postpone _____

8. companion _____

9. submarine _____

10. combine _____

© Macmillan/McGraw-Hill

Name _____

A. Fill in each blank with a vocabulary word.

Renaissance	philosopher	elaborate	recommend
commissioned	miniature	envisioned	proportion

1. A _____, such as Socrates or René Descartes, is a person who asks and sometimes answers questions about life.

2. During the _____, which began in Italy, many famous works of art were made for royalty.

3. Leonardo da Vinci _____ many great works of art and then painted them on canvas.

4. Da Vinci studied the _____ of the human body, or the relation of its parts to each other and to the whole.

5. Some master painters made _____ and highly detailed paintings.

6. I _____ that you look through the art books in the library to see some of them.

7. An architect was _____ to design a new room for the queen's palace.

8. The king has a tiny _____ sculpture of da Vinci.

B. Use two of the vocabulary words in sentences of your own.

9. _____

_____

10. _____

_____

R 1.0 Word Analysis, Fluency, and Systematic Vocabulary Development

© Macmillan/McGraw-Hill

Name _____

A **generalization** is a broad statement based on a number of
details. Generalizations contain words such as *all, always, often,
many, most, more, less, none,* or *least.* A good generalization
cannot be proved false.

**Read the passage. Then read the generalizations that follow and
tell whether each is valid. If a generalization is valid, underline the
signal word or words in it.**

Before the invention of the printing press, books were hard to obtain in
Europe. Books had to be copied by hand, which took a long time and was
expensive. Most books were bibles or prayer books and were owned by a
church. Books were often written in Latin, even though people did not speak
Latin in their daily lives. Most people were illiterate, or could not read. They
did not have books to learn to read. When the printing press was invented,
books became less expensive. They began to be printed in English, French,
and German. Literacy rates increased.

1. Before the invention of the printing press, all books were written in Latin.

   _____

2. Even though most books were printed in Latin, people did not speak Latin in

   their daily lives. _____

3. It was less expensive to produce all books by hand than to produce them on

   a printing press. _____

4. Most people were illiterate or could not read, because they did not have

   books. _____

5. After books were printed in English, French, and German, more people

   learned to read. _____

© Macmillan/McGraw-Hill

 R 2.0 Reading Comprehension (Focus on Informational Materials)

As you read *Leonardo's Horse*, fill in the Generalizations Chart.

Important Information	Generalization

How does the information you wrote in this Generalizations Chart help
you monitor comprehension of *Leonardo's Horse*?

© Macmillan/McGraw-Hill

R 2.0 Reading Comprehension (Focus on Informational Materials)

As I read, I will pay attention to intonation and phrasing.

9	Michelangelo's family had deep roots in the city of
18	Florence. His mother, Francesca, was related to a very
25	powerful man. He was Lorenzo de Medici (MED-uh-chee),
32	who ruled the city. Michelangelo's father, Lodovico
39	(loh-doh-VEE-koh), came from a long line of government
49	officials. But at the time Michelangelo was born, the family
58	wasn't doing well. Money was scarce. Yet Lodovico refused
71	to get a regular job. He thought of himself as a gentleman. In
82	those days, gentlemen didn't work, at least not with their hands.
92	The family was saved when Lodovico became mayor of a
98	small village called Caprese (kah-PRAY-zay). Lodovico and
111	his family moved into a simple stone house and began a new life.
119	Early in the morning of March 6, 1475, Francesca gave
128	birth to her second child. They named him Michelangelo.
139	When Michelangelo was still a baby, his father lost his job.
149	The family decided to return to Florence. His mother was
162	very ill at the time. She could not care for her infant son.
174	So she left him with a stonecutter and his wife. The couple
187	lived in a nearby village. Most of the men in this village were
	also stonecutters. 189

Comprehension Check

1. Why were stonecutters not considered gentlemen? **Make Generalizations**

2. How do you know that a person's social position at this time was important?
Make Inferences

	Words Read	–	Number of Errors	=	Words Correct Score
First Read		–		=	
Second Read		–		=	

© Macmillan/McGraw-Hill

R 1.1 Read aloud narrative and expository text fluently and accurately
and with appropriate pacing, **intonation**, and expression.

When you research a topic, you will often need to consult **primary sources**, such as journals and diaries, that come from the time and place you are researching.

The following excerpt is from a sailor's journal. After you read the passage, answer the questions.

September 1, 1724. Sailed day and night west, fourteen leagues. Four tropical birds came to the ship, which is a very clear sign of land, for so many birds of one sort together show that we are not lost. Twice, saw two pelicans; many weeds. The constellation called Las Gallardias, which at evening appeared in a westerly direction, was seen in the northeast the next morning, making no more progress in a night of nine hours. This was the case every night, as says the Admiral. At night the needles varied a point towards the northwest. In the morning they were true, by which it appears that the polar star moves, like the others, and the needles are always right.

1. What kind of information does the journal give?

   _____

   _____

2. Why might this primary source be useful?

   _____

   _____

3. What do you learn about life on the ship?

   _____

   _____

4. How much distance did the ship travel in the time covered in this journal entry?

   _____

© Macmillan/McGraw-Hill

 R 2.1 Identify the structural features of popular media (e.g., newspapers, magazines, online information) and use the features to obtain information.

Words are often made up of parts, including prefixes, suffixes, and roots or base words. Knowing the meanings of **Greek roots** will help you expand your vocabulary.

A. Identify the Greek roots of each of the words. Write the root(s) and meaning on the line provided. Use a dictionary to help.

1. telegram: _____

2. cosmopolitan: _____

3. chronology: _____

4. autograph: _____

5. bibliography: _____

B. Use each of the words above in a sentence of your own.

6. _____

_____

7. _____

_____

8. _____

_____

9. _____

_____

10. _____

_____

CA **R 1.0** Word Analysis, Fluency, and Systematic Vocabulary Development

Using the Word Study Steps

1. LOOK at the word.

2. SAY the word aloud.

3. STUDY the letters in the word.

4. WRITE the word.

5. CHECK the word.
   Did you spell the word right?
   If not, go back to step 1.

Find Rhyming Words

Circle the word in each row that does not rhyme with the spelling word on the left.

1. **interfere**	cavalry	volunteer	pioneer
2. **transform**	reform	storm	alarm
3. **interrupt**	abrupt	corrupt	script
4. **profession**	admission	obsession	discretion
5. **proportion**	distortion	emotion	contortion
6. **postwar**	beware	décor	explore
7. **transfer**	answer	dancer	sister
8. **submit**	transmit	allot	permit
9. **commission**	contortion	tradition	ambition
10. **submarine**	routine	shine	caffeine
11. **combine**	assign	decline	fringe
12. **transparent**	clearance	parent	apparent
13. **intersection**	direction	temptation	perfection
14. **postpone**	cyclone	alone	crown
15. **transformation**	vacation	selection	sensation

© Macmillan/McGraw-Hill

 LC 1.5 Spell roots, suffixes, prefixes, contractions, and syllable constructions correctly.

Name _____

A. There are five spelling mistakes in the paragraph below. Circle the misspelled words. Write the words correctly on the lines below.

   Each year, the Martin Luther King Jr. Middle School holds a design competition. Imani and her companyon Bartholomew decided to work together for the competition. They wanted to design a playground for their community in a suberb of New York City. They knew if they could coperate and comebine their talents they would have a good chance of winning. They were eager to submitt their design. They were even happier to find out that they had won.

1. _____   2. _____   3. _____

4. _____   5. _____

Writing Activity

B. Were you ever really excited to find out that you had won something? Write a letter to a friend explaining how you felt after you had won. Use five spelling words.

_____

_____

_____

_____

_____

_____

_____

_____

_____

_____

_____

LC 1.5 Spell roots, suffixes, prefixes, contractions, and syllable constructions correctly.

Name _____

> • Use a plural verb with a plural **indefinite pronoun**, such as *both*, *few*, *many*, *others*, or *several*.

Read each sentence. Choose the verb in parentheses that correctly completes the sentence and write it on the line provided.

1. Many of us (enjoys, enjoy) cycling. _____

2. A few (rides, ride) every morning. _____

3. Both Sam and Sally (wishes, wish) to win the cycling tournament.

   _____

4. Several riders (trains, train) with a coach. _____

5. Others (likes, like) to train on their own. _____

Circle the indefinite pronoun. Write S if the indefinite pronoun is singular. Write P if the indefinite pronoun is plural.

6. A few of the riders wear special riding gloves. _____

7. Others have special riding helmets. _____

8. Somebody is here from the newspaper to cover the story.

   _____

9. The reporter said there was something exciting about every race.

   _____

10. Many cannot get seats and are standing on the grass. _____

LC 1.2 Identify and properly use indefinite pronouns and present perfect, past perfect, and future perfect verb tenses; ensure that verbs agree with compound subjects.

- An **indefinite pronoun** does not refer to a particular person, place, or thing.
- Use a singular verb with a singular indefinite pronoun, such as *anybody, anyone, anything, each, everybody, everyone, everything, nobody, nothing, somebody, someone,* or *something.*
- Use a plural verb with a plural indefinite pronoun, such as *both, few, many, others,* or *several.*

Proofread this news article. Then rewrite the article using the correct singular or plural verbs. Correct any mistakes in punctuation.

Samantha Higgins, a twelve-year-old sixth grader from Memphis, Tennessee, won the 30K Cycling Championship today in this city. Many fans believes that Samantha who completed the race in record time had an advantage with her clipless pedals. Clipless pedals locks into a cleat in the sole of a special cycling shoe. When asked what other tips she have for riders, Samantha said "Everybody must checks cadence. Few winning riders ignores maintenance. Everyone must cleans, lubes, and checks the bike! Nobody should rides without a helmet. Ever."

_____

_____

_____

_____

_____

_____

_____

_____

_____

LC 1.2 Identify and properly use indefinite pronouns and present perfect, past perfect, and future perfect verb tenses; ensure that verbs agree with compound subjects.

Name _____

1. *All schools should require students to wear uniforms.*

2. *Schools should not require students to wear uniforms.*

3. *Schools should only serve and sell healthy food.*

4. *Schools should sell and serve a variety of food, and students should decide what they want to eat.*

1. Read the definitions of credible evidence and reliable evidence.

   Definitions:

   Credible evidence: believable and worthy of confidence

   Reliable evidence: trustworthy and dependable

2. Read the list of statements/arguments at the top of the page. Consider whether you have personal evidence to support any of these statements. Now think about whether you have information from outside sources to support any of these statements.

3. Choose one of the following statements/arguments from that list at the top of the page. Write 4–6 sentences of evidence to support that claim/assertion. Circle the personal evidence that you write. Underline the information from outside sources, if you use any of that kind of evidence.

_____

_____

_____

_____

_____

_____

_____

_____

_____

_____

_____

© Macmillan/McGraw-Hill

Sometimes the end **consonant** sound of a base word changes with the addition of suffixes.

a. Words that end with a hard **c** often change to the soft **c** sound with the addition of particular suffixes. For example, the hard **c** of **physic** turns to a soft **c** in **physician**. However, it stays hard in **physical**.

b. Words that end in a soft **c** often change to make the **/sh/** sound with the addition of the **-ial** suffix. For example, the soft **c** in **office** changes to **/sh/** in **official**.

c. Words that end in **-ct** change the **/t/** sound to **/sh/** with the addition of the **-ion** suffix. For example, the **/t/** in **select** changes to **/sh/** in **selection**.

A. Read each sentence and underline the word that has a consonant alternation with the addition of a suffix. Write the base word. Then write *a*, *b*, or *c*, depending on which of the above rules the word follows.

1. The facial carvings of the masks are amazing. _____

2. I feel a strong attraction to the history of art. _____

3. The columnist criticized the exhibit at the museum. _____

4. The construction of the exhibit took weeks to finish. _____

5. I am interested in the medicine men of South American Indians.

_____

B. Choose three of the underlined words from the five sentences above. Write one sentence of your own for each of the words you chose.

6. _____

7. _____

8. _____

Name _____

A. Fill in each blank with a vocabulary word.

inscribed	resemblance	substitutes	enthralled
regulation	grouchy	embarrassment	capacity

Our quiz team would never have won the prize without working together. At our first practice, everyone was _____ because it was so early in the morning. Jenny suffered from _____ because she forgot the answers to most of the science questions. Hiroshi was _____ with the buzzers. Keila refused to wear the _____ uniform. Our _____ did not show up. Finally, our coach opened a letter. _____ on the envelope was the name of my favorite game-show host. He had written to our coach for advice when he was young. Our coach explained that we had no chance of winning if we did not have even a _____ to a team. We had the _____ to win, but we needed team spirit! Once we found it, we were able to cooperate and to win.

B. Choose two vocabulary words. Write sentences using these words.

1. _____

_____

2. _____

_____

_____

 R 1.0 Word Analysis, Fluency, and Systematic Vocabulary Development

© Macmillan/McGraw-Hill

Read the story and answer the questions.

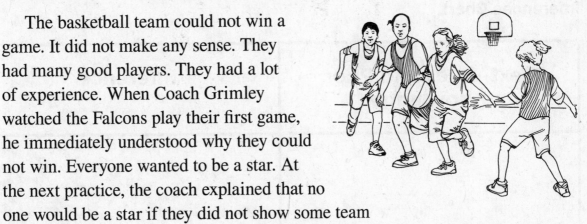

The basketball team could not win a game. It did not make any sense. They had many good players. They had a lot of experience. When Coach Grimley watched the Falcons play their first game, he immediately understood why they could not win. Everyone wanted to be a star. At the next practice, the coach explained that no one would be a star if they did not show some team spirit and support each other. In practices during the next week, all the team members did was pass the ball to other players who were in a better position to score points. When the next game came around, the Falcons won!

1. Why could the Falcons not win?

_____

_____

2. What is implied by the sentence, "Everyone wanted to be a star"?

_____

_____

3. What can you infer about Coach Grimley's approach to basketball?

_____

_____

4. What can you infer from the Falcons' winning?

_____

_____

R 2.0 Reading Comprehension (Focus on Informational Materials)

As you read *How Tía Lola Came to Visit/Stay*, fill in the
Inferences Chart.

Text Clues and Prior Knowledge	Inference

How does the information you wrote in this Inferences Chart help you
better understand *How Tía Lola Came to Visit/Stay*?

CA R 2.0 Reading Comprehension (Focus on Informational Materials)

© Macmillan/McGraw-Hill

Name _____

As I read, I will pay attention to intonation and phrasing.

	Jenna turns her head to look at the pennant on the wall
12	above her bed. It's from her old school basketball team, the
23	Wilson Wildcats. Jenna had been a star forward on the team,
34	and some of her best friends had played, too. Then again,
45	Jenna had had a lot of friends at Wilson. She had lived in
58	the same small town her whole life. Being at Wilson was like
70	going to school with your extended family.
77	Now Jenna, her brother, Sean, and her parents had moved
87	into a new neighborhood in a big city. There were three times
99	as many students at Eastern Middle School as there were at
110	Wilson. Jenna let out a loud sigh. How was she ever going to
123	make friends?
125	After dinner the night before the first day, Jenna and
135	Sean play one-on-one basketball in the driveway.
144	They've been shooting baskets together as long as Jenna can
154	remember. Their evening games have always been Jenna's
162	favorite part of the day. 167

Comprehension Check

1. What kind of relationship do Jenna and her brother have? **Make Inferences**

2. Why was Wilson like an extended family for Jenna? **Cause and Effect**

	Words Read	–	Number of Errors	=	Words Correct Score
First Read		–		=	
Second Read		–		=	

© Macmillan/McGraw-Hill

R 1.1 Read aloud narrative and expository text fluently and accurately and with appropriate pacing, **intonation**, and expression.

Name _____

An **almanac** contains general information about various topics. Almanacs are published yearly and contain statistics for the previous year.

Almanacs are filled with up-to-date information in a concise format. The index is the organizer for the almanac. Almanacs also appear online and they often have indexes that are links to the information you are seeking.

Use the almanac index to answer the questions.

Animals	First Aid	Mortality Statistics	Taxes
Architecture	Foreign Phrases	Newspapers	Time Zones
Baseball	Geography	Nutrition	Tropical Storms
Calendars	Governors, U.S.	Olympics	Volcanoes
Cities, World	Holidays	Presidents	Weather
Endangered Species	Hurricanes	Refugees	Writing/Language

1. Under which three headings would you probably find information about Hurricane Andrew? _____

2. Where could you learn the days of the week in French?

_____

3. Where could you find out who designed a famous building?

_____

4. Where would you find out what public official is the head of your state?

_____

5. Where could you find out what time it is in Sydney, Australia?

_____

6. Which two headings might have information about bald eagles?

_____

 R 2.1 Identify the structural features of popular media (e.g., newspapers, magazines, online information) and use the features to obtain information.

Name _____

Change each sentence to the past tense by adding the inflectional ending *-ed* to appropriate action verbs.

1. Kim and Joey play together after school on Mondays.

_____

_____

2. The class members work together to decorate the gym.

_____

_____

3. Even though they fail to win the game, the players hope to win the next one.

_____

_____

4. Every person creates a part of the presentation.

_____

5. When we walk on a school trip, we cross the street together as a class.

_____

_____

6. Jamal helps his friends build a model car.

_____

7. Jumanda saves her money to buy a new computer.

_____

8. Yoshi likes to read aloud in class.

_____

Name _____

Using the Word Study Steps

1. LOOK at the word.

2. SAY the word aloud.

3. STUDY the letters in the word.

4. WRITE the word.

5. CHECK the word.
   Did you spell the word right?
   If not, go back to step 1.

Find the Words

Find and circle the spelling words hidden in each set of letters.

1. m a k i c r e a t e n a t e l y   _____

2. p u b l i c i t r e j e c i a l   _____

3. p u b p r e j u d i c i a l e t e   _____

4. m u s c u l s o l e m n a t e   _____

5. p r e j u d i c e a t i o n   _____

6. c r e a t c r u m b i l i o n   _____

7. d e s i n g i n g o f f i c i a l   _____

8. m u s c u l a r e a l i t r a t e   _____

9. p r e d e s i g n a t i l i t y   _____

10. o f f i c e a l a r p u b i a t e   _____

11. s o l e m m u s c l e a t l y   _____

12. r e j e c r e j e c t i n a l i c e   _____

13. c r u m a g i c a b l e u l a r   _____

14. c r e a t i o n o f f i c u l a t e   _____

LC 1.5 Spell frequently misspelled words correctly
(e.g., *their, they're, there*).

© Macmillan/McGraw-Hill

Name ____________________

A. Proofreading

There are five spelling mistakes in the paragraph below. Circle the misspelled words. Write the words correctly on the lines below.

One day during the summer, Maxwell sat in the park with a group of friends and showed them the new magick tricks he had learned. His friends were impressed with his new skills, and soon a crowd of people had formed to watch Maxwell perform. Maxwell decided that this would be a good way to spend his summer. He decided to dezignate a specific place and time each day when he would perform his show. To make it oficial, he asked his sister to help him dezine a poster. The poster said "Every day at 4:00 on the Great Lawn in Panorama Park come witness the amazing talents of Maxwell the Master Magition."

1. ____________ **2.** ____________ **3.** ____________

4. ____________ **5.** ____________

B. Writing Activity

Have you ever turned your talents into a rewarding job? Write a story about a talent that you would like to use in your career. Use at least five spelling words.

____

____

____

____

____

____

____

____

____

____

© Macmillan/McGraw-Hill

CA **LC 1.5** Spell frequently misspelled words correctly (e.g., *their, they're, there*).

Name _____

> • Verbs must agree with indefinite **pronouns**.

Rewrite each sentence, choosing the verb in parentheses that agrees with the indefinite pronoun.

1. Everything (is, are) incredibly interesting at an archaeological dig.

   _____

   _____

2. No one (deny, denies) that the work is extremely difficult.

   _____

3. Both of the archaeologists (work, works) at a major university.

   _____

4. A few of the volunteers (is, are) students at the school.

   _____

5. Nobody (make, makes) much money as a volunteer on a dig.

   _____

6. Everyone (know, knows) that the pleasure is in the possibility of discovery.

   _____

   _____

7. Others (claim, claims) that they most enjoy the countries they get to visit.

   _____

   _____

8. (Do, Does) anybody want to volunteer for a dig in Arizona?

   _____

9. Many (have, has) already signed up.

   _____

10. Several (want, wants) to sign up for the dig in Oregon.

    _____

 LC 1.0 Written and Oral English Language Conventions

Name _____

- A verb must agree with its subject **pronoun**.

Pronouns	Verbs
he, she, it	walks, is, was, has
we, you, they	walk, are, were, have
I	walk, am, was, have

- Verbs must also agree with indefinite pronouns.
- Use a singular verb with a singular indefinite pronoun.
- Use a plural verb with a plural indefinite pronoun.

Proofread this magazine article. Then rewrite the article, making sure verbs agree with subject nouns and pronouns. Correct any mistakes in punctuation.

During the third century B.C., people who lived in the lands between the Tigris and Euphrates rivers founding the first cities. These people invents writing. They also creates architecture develops irrigation writes poetry and makes laws. They was an amazing civilization. Can anybody sees the art of the Sumerians and not marvel? Several works of art is on display this month at our local history museum. Everyone should visits.

_____

_____

_____

_____

_____

_____

© Macmillan/McGraw-Hill

1. According to an article published in The New York Times, *communities around the Mojave Desert are at a high risk of earthquakes.*

   Seems reliable because:

   Seems unreliable because:

2. *Many teachers left New Orleans after Hurricane Katrina and never came back, explained Senator Barack Obama to a first grade class in New Orleans on the second anniversary of the storm, August, 2007.*

   Seems reliable because:

   Seems unreliable because:

3. *My friend Denise wrote in a birthday card that she gave me in December, 2006 that I am the best friend she ever had.*

   Seems reliable because:

   Seems unreliable because:

1. Read the statements at the top of the page.
2. Underline the source in each sentence.
3. For each sentence, explain what it is about this source that makes it seem reliable.
4. For each sentence, explain what it is about this source that makes it NOT seem reliable.

© Macmillan/McGraw-Hill

 W 1.0 Writing Strategies

Homophones are words that sound alike but are spelled differently. These words are examples of the fact that different letters and combinations of letters can stand for the same sound.

For example, the homophone of *principal* is spelled *principle*. Both the *-al* and the *-le* make the /əl/ sound.

A. Use each pair of clues to find the homophones. Make sure you spell the different words correctly.

1. two plus two / a preposition indicating purpose _____

2. a spoken or written story / a cat has one _____

3. the selling of something at a low price / a piece of cloth that helps move a boat _____

4. take a survey / a long cylinder _____

5. heaviness / remain in readiness _____

6. plant / use a needle and thread _____

7. the opposite of old / had an understanding of _____

8. a soldier who wore armor / the opposite of day _____

B. Write sentences using four of the homophones from above.

9. _____

_____

10. _____

_____

11. _____

_____

12. _____

_____

R 1.0 Word Analysis, Fluency, and Systematic Vocabulary Development

Name _____

| modern | erupt | ancient | reclaim |
| billow | crater | active | energy |

A. Complete each sentence by using the best word from the box.

1. Unlike early scientists, _____ volcano watchers have the advantage of using high technology.

2. Having erupted several times since 1980, Mount St. Helens is one of the most _____ volcanoes in the United States.

3. The _____ city of Pompeii was destroyed by a volcano in AD 79.

4. In 1975, residents of Washington State saw clouds of steam and smoke _____ from Mount Baker.

5. A tiltmeter is one of the devices that scientists can use to predict when a volcano may be ready to _____.

6. Lava from the volcano destroyed acres of forest, but trees are slowly beginning to _____ areas of the slope.

7. In some volcanic areas, people use underground steam as a source of _____.

8. In Hawai'i Volcanoes National Park, visitors can drive around the rim of a bowl-shaped volcanic _____.

B. Choose two of the vocabulary words in the box above and write a sentence for each.

9. _____

_____

10. _____

_____

© Macmillan/McGraw-Hill

Name _____

As I read, I will pay attention to pronunciation.

	During the Middle Ages, most people in Europe were
9	farmers. They lived in villages on the estate of a noble. They
21	grew crops and tended animals. They provided food for
30	themselves and others. They also had to make by hand
40	everything they wore or used. There were no machines.
49	At the same time, many men and women were skilled in
60	various crafts. One person in a village, for instance, might
70	be a weaver. Other villagers went to him or her for wool and
83	linen cloth to make into clothing. Villagers also needed a
93	carpenter to build their houses. They needed a blacksmith to
103	make iron tools and nails.
108	As time passed, more people needed the things made by
118	these craftspeople, such as cloth and tools. So some people
128	stopped farming and worked at their craft. People began
137	to depend on the work of skilled craftspeople. The
146	craftspeople became more specialized, and the number of
154	different crafts grew. Medieval craftspeople made everything
161	from arrows and armor to wheels and woolen cloth. 170

Comprehension Check

1. Find at least three words in the passage that are homophones. List them along with their homophones. **Homophones**

2. Why does the author write about the craftspeople? **Author's Purpose**

	Words Read	–	Number of Errors	=	Words Correct Score
First Read		–		=	
Second Read		–		=	

R 1.1 Read aloud narrative and expository text fluently and accurately and with appropriate pacing, intonation, and expression.

A myth is a traditional story that explains imaginary events from the past or a traditional world view. Myths describe how a custom, belief, or natural phenomenon came about. **Symbolism** is the use of concrete objects to represent abstract ideas or qualities. **Figurative language** uses imaginative language to describe objects, places, or people.

Read the myth below, then answer the questions.

A long time ago there was one land and one people. Everyone lived together happily and in peace. Then two brothers were born who quarreled over everything. This made the Creator angry. In a voice like low, rumbling thunder, he told the brothers to shoot an arrow into the air. Each brother and his people would live where his arrow landed.

Soon the brothers started quarreling again. Once more the Creator became angry. This time he took away fire from everyone except for one old woman called Loo-Wit. The people stopped quarreling, and the Creator asked Loo-Wit to share her fire. In return, the Creator offered to grant her one wish. She chose to be young and beautiful. When the two brothers saw how beautiful Loo-Wit was, each of them wanted to marry her. Again there was quarreling, which caused the Creator to turn each brother into a mountain and also to make Loo-Wit a mountain.

1. The myth says that the brothers shot their arrows into the air. What does this explain? _____

_____

2. What do the mountains symbolize? _____

_____

3. Find an example of figurative language in the myth.

_____

 R 3.7 Explain the effects of common literary devices (e.g., symbolism, imagery, metaphor) in a variety of fictional and nonfictional texts.

Each entry word in a thesaurus is followed by a list of synonyms.
The synonyms have almost the same meaning, but they often have
different shades of meaning. For example, two synonyms listed for the
word *angry* might be *annoyed* and *infuriated*. Both mean "angry," but
infuriated has a much stronger meaning than *annoyed*.

**A. For each word below, use your thesaurus to find two synonyms,
one with a weaker meaning, and one with a stronger meaning.
Write them on the lines.**

1. tired

Weaker synonym: _____

Stronger synonym: _____

3. cold

Weaker synonym: _____

Stronger synonym: _____

2. drop

Weaker synonym: _____

Stronger synonym: _____

4. large

Weaker synonym: _____

Stronger synonym: _____

**B. Choose one pair of synonyms you wrote above. Write a sentence for
each.**

5. _____

_____

6. _____

_____

R 1.5 Understand and explain "shades of meaning" in related words
(e.g., *softly* and *quietly*).

Name _____

Using the Word Study Steps

1. LOOK at the word.

2. SAY the word aloud.

3. STUDY the letters in the word.

4. WRITE the word.

5. CHECK the word.
   Did you spell the word right?
   If not, go back to step 1.

Find the Words

Find and circle the spelling words in the puzzle below.

```
A R P R I N C I P L E B C A
P W L E S S O N A C R E A B
R A V A L M H C A P C E L D
I N A V E I N I J R O K N L
A C L A M N O V A I N O A P
I R E L R O S A I N S O V O
S H E E R R E N ' C T R E N
L U R S I ' L E L I D O L R
E S V S V A R A R P S T E V
L S A E M P P T P A N E A R
E H R N A V A L O L S A L A
V E R E H S I D L E R A H M
I A A A M I N E R R I ' L L
L R O N O L A F E S V R E L
```

LC 1.5 Spell frequently misspelled words correctly
(e.g., *their, they're, there*).

A. Proofreading Activity

There are five spelling mistakes in the paragraph below. Circle the misspelled words. Write the words correctly on the line below.

Of all the important people in Zhora's life, her elementary school principle, Mr. Reiner, was one of the most influential. Mr. Reiner taught Zhora one very important lessen in life—the importance of working hard and not being idel. Mr. Reiner explained that life can be difficult and pain is inevitable, but to remain focused on your goals and persistently work towards them. Zhora will always rememember Mr. Reiner's poignant words, and considers him her idoll.

1. _____   2. _____   3. _____

4. _____   5. _____

B. Writing Activity

Is there someone in your life who once gave you some really important advice? Write a letter to that person thanking them for the wisdom they bestowed upon you. Use five spelling words.

_____

_____

_____

_____

_____

_____

_____

_____

_____

_____

LC 1.5 Spell frequently misspelled words correctly
(e.g., *their, they're, there*).

Volcanoes • Grade 6/Unit 5   261

Name _____

Practice

Grammar:
Adjectives and
Demonstrative
Adjectives

- A **demonstrative adjective** points out something and tells *which one* or *which ones.*
- Use *this* and *that* with singular nouns. Use *these* and *those* with plural nouns.
- *This* and *these* refer to nouns that are nearby; *that* and *those* refer to nouns that are farther away.

A. Study the demonstrative adjectives in parentheses. Write the demonstrative adjective that correctly completes each sentence on the line provided.

1. _____ essay is mine. (These, This)

2. The students must read _____ books for English class. (these, this)

3. _____ book is about a traveling family. (These, That)

4. Will you hand me _____ theater tickets? (those, that)

5. _____ essay got the highest grade in the class. (This, Those)

B. Complete each sentence with an appropriate demonstrative adjective.

6. Please get me _____ book on the highest shelf.

7. _____ are the oranges Juni likes best.

8. _____ is the novel that we will be reading.

9. _____ oranges are the sweetest in the store.

10. _____ is the dress I want to wear tonight.

© Macmillan/McGraw-Hill

CA **LC 1.0** Written and Oral English Language Conventions

- An **adjective** is a word that modifies, or describes, a noun or pronoun and tells *what kind, how many,* or *which one.*
- A **predicate adjective** follows a linking verb and describes the subject.
- A **demonstrative adjective** points out something and tells *which one* or *which ones.*
- A **proper adjective** is formed from a proper noun. Begin a proper adjective with a capital letter.

Proofread this speech. Then rewrite the speech, correcting any errors in the use of predicate, demonstrative, or proper adjectives. Correct any mistakes in the use of homophones, capitalization, or punctuation.

This mourning we honor Mr. Tyburn, whose retiring after forty years of teaching english at our middle school. I was fortunate to have this wonderful teacher last year in sixth grade. His guidance was crucial in encouraging me to read more and right more. He opened up the world of american literature to me. Because of Mr. Tyburn, I am planning on a career as a journalist. My mentor Mr. Tyburn arranged for me to work as an intern at our local newspaper. Thank you Mr. Tyburn for all your hard work and encouragement.

_____

_____

_____

_____

_____

_____

_____

_____

_____

Name _____

"Peanut Butter Rule"
By Hannah Johnson

There shouldn't be a rule at school that nobody can bring peanut butter. Lots of people like peanut butter so much that they would bring it every day if they could. What are those people supposed to bring for lunch, jelly sandwiches? If you're allergic to peanut butter, have something else. But just because some people can't eat it, it isn't fair to take it away from everyone.

"Danger Zone"
By Andy Burke

Thousands of students in this country find their lives in danger when they walk into the school cafeteria. Allergies are on the rise in this country, and school cafeterias are the new "danger zone"! Although it is hard to believe, many children (some as young as kindergarten) are SO allergic to peanut butter that if they sit near someone with a peanut butter sandwich, they may need to be rushed to the hospital! Are peanut butter sandwiches SO important to students that they would risk putting a kindergartner in the hospital? It may not be everyone's favorite choice, but the decision to keep school cafeterias "nut-free" is SAFE FOR EVERYONE.

1. **Read** the two arguments at the top of the page.

2. **Underline** the lead in each argument.

3. **Think:** Which lead catches your attention? Why?

4. **Read** this argument:

   Schools should not sell fast food in the cafeteria or in any vending machines.

5. **Think:** How could you get someone's attention about this argument?

6. **Write** two different leads for the cafeteria vending machine argument. (Do not write the whole paragraph—just write the leads).

1. _____

2. _____

Extra Practice: Write another style of lead for this argument. OR Re-write the leads for the two arguments at the top of the page.

© Macmillan/McGraw-Hill

 W 1.0 Writing Strategies

The English language borrows many **words from around the world**. Some of the words are cognates, or spelled and pronounced almost the same way as they are in the original language. Others are words made of foreign phrases. Knowing a word's original meaning can help you understand and remember it.

A. Use a dictionary to find the original language and meaning of each word.

1. gong _____

_____

2. algebra _____

_____

3. pizza _____

4. typhoon _____

5. bazaar _____

6. denim _____

_____

7. bronco _____

8. sombrero _____

9. caribou _____

10. igloo _____

B. Choose two of the words above and write a sentence for each one.

11. _____

_____

12. _____

_____

A. Each vocabulary word is shown in context in the sentences below. Circle the context clues as you read 1–8.

dwelling	ambitious	lounge	pondering
drowsy	revived	agonized	vapors

1. Mateo's house, or <u>dwelling,</u> was in the path of the volcano.

2. Caitlin was an <u>ambitious</u> girl: She wanted to be successful.

3. Carlin did not waste time and <u>lounge</u> around in an unproductive way.

4. Juanita spent her afternoon <u>pondering</u> her schedule, thinking about what to do next.

5. This medicine might make you feel <u>drowsy</u>, or sleepy.

6. A good night's sleep <u>revived</u> the weary traveler and energized him.

7. Kim <u>agonized</u> and suffered over her decision.

8. She knew if the volcano erupted, the <u>vapors</u> would be gases and debris.

B. Use the context clues to write the definition of each vocabulary word on the line provided.

9. dwelling _____

10. ambitious _____

11. lounge _____

12. pondering _____

13. drowsy _____

14. revived _____

15. agonized _____

16. vapors _____

CA R 1.0 Word Analysis, Fluency, and Systematic Vocabulary Development

The **theme** is the main idea of a story. Authors often do not state the theme directly. They reveal it through the interaction of the characters, or in actions, or conflict. The theme can usually be summed up in one sentence. For instance, consider the story of the tortoise and the hare. In this well-known story, the tortoise and the hare are in a race. Of course, the hare can run very fast, and everyone (especially the hare) is sure that he will win the race. The tortoise cannot run at all, and walks very, very slowly. But the hare is overconfident, and he stops to rest between spurts. The tortoise continues on his way, slowly but surely, and reaches the finish line first. The theme of the story, never directly stated by the author, is "Slow and steady wins the race."

Read the passage below.

The ground was shaking from the earthquake as Melvin stood outside his apartment building at the end of the street. His mother stood next to him and silently grabbed his hand. Melvin looked at her and realized they were totally unprepared. What should they do? Where could they go? Melvin had no idea. He looked back into the apartment building and then at his mother. He realized that everything they had—all their furniture, pots and pans, and clothing—meant nothing unless he and his mother lived through this awful day. He turned back to her and said, "We can run very fast if we take nothing."

Circle the theme that best states the main idea or message of the story.

When trouble comes, people reach out to help each other.

When trouble comes, people realize what they value most in life.

When trouble comes, people show their worst traits because they are afraid.

 R 2.0 Reading Comprehension (Focus on Informational Materials)

As you read *The Dog of Pompeii*, fill in the Theme Chart.

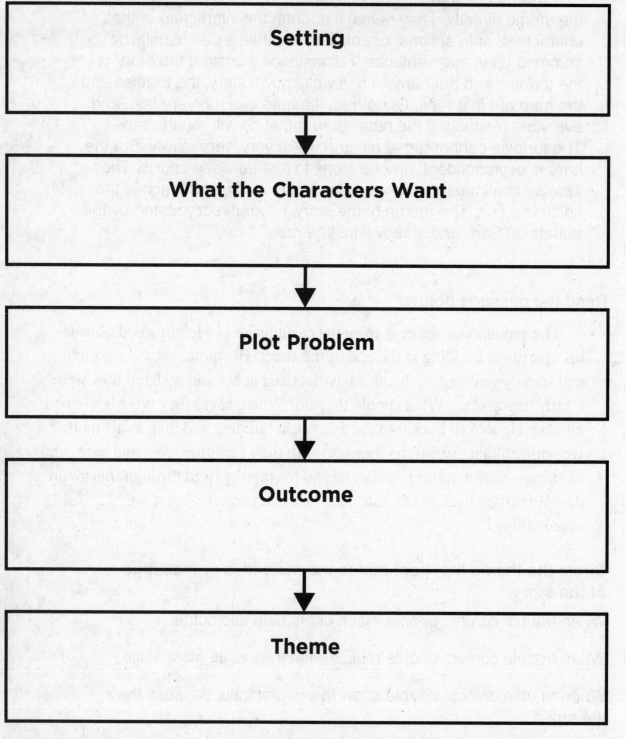

Setting

What the Characters Want

Plot Problem

Outcome

Theme

© Macmillan/McGraw-Hill

How does the information you wrote in this Theme Chart help you better
understand *The Dog of Pompeii*?

CA **R 2.0** Reading Comprehension (Focus on Informational Materials)

Name _____

As I read, I will pay attention to intonation and phrasing.

11	"What do you figure Pa'll bring back from his trip?" Seth asked Jed.
13	"He's bound to bring back news about what's happening in
23	the rest of the world. And you know he'll have a tall tale about his
38	adventures at the trading post," answered Jed, chuckling.
46	"Do you remember the story about the time the syrup trapped
57	him?" giggled Seth.
60	"As I recollect," recounted Jed, "Pa said he'd been doing a fair
72	bit of **pondering** at the trading post, trying to decide which of the
85	fabrics Ma would like for a new dress and which ones he should
98	buy for the little ones' smocks. He was mighty tired looking at all
111	those bolts of cloth, so he leaned his elbows on the counter,
123	looking left, right, up, and down, over and over, until finally he'd
135	made his decisions. But when he tried to stand up, he couldn't
147	budge! His elbows were stuck in a pool of syrup that he hadn't
160	noticed was on the counter."
165	"And the syrup had hardened by the time Pa wanted to stand
177	up, so he felt like a beetle trapped in pitch," finished Seth, nearly
190	convulsed with laughter. "Do you remember how Pa showed us
200	what had happened to him?" 205

Comprehension Check

1. What happens while Pa is at the trading post? **Summarize**

2. Why do you think Pa tells his children tall tales? **Make Inferences**

	Words Read	–	Number of Errors	=	Words Correct Score
First Read		–		=	
Second Read		–		=	

© Macmillan/McGraw-Hill

CA **R 1.1** Read aloud narrative and expository text fluently and accurately and with appropriate pacing, **intonation**, and expression.

The Dog of Pompeii • Grade 6/Unit 5   **269**

Name _____

Graphic aids can help you understand processes and events. Graphic aids include diagrams, charts, tables, illustrations, graphs, and photographs. Graphic aids should help you better understand the text they accompany and should provide additional information.

How a Volcano Forms

When a volcano erupts, lava and other materials flow onto Earth's surface. The materials pile up around the opening as they cool. Over time a mountain may form. Both the opening and the mountain around it are called a *volcano*.

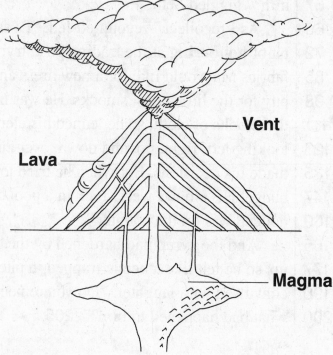

Vent

Lava

Magma

Use the diagram to answer the questions.

1. What is shown in the diagram? _____
   _____

2. What is the part of the volcano through which the lava erupts? _____
   _____

3. What causes the mountain part of the volcano to form? _____
   _____

4. What is lava called before it erupts? _____
   _____

© Macmillan/McGraw-Hill

CA **R 2.0** Reading Comprehension (Focus on Informational Materials)

Multiple-meaning words have more than one meaning. Context will often allow you to determine which meaning of a word is being used.

Example: I went to the <u>lounge</u> to get a bottle of water.
I <u>lounge</u> about all day on Saturdays.

In the first example, the word *lounge* refers to a "place to get refreshments." In the second sentence, *lounge* means "relax."

Each of the following words has more than one meaning. Write at least one sentence for each meaning of the word.

1. content _____

   content _____

2. frank _____

   frank _____

3. lark _____

   lark _____

4. mount _____

   mount _____

5. paddle _____

   paddle _____

6. object _____

   object _____

7. conductor _____

   conductor _____

8. fine _____

   fine _____

© Macmillan/McGraw-Hill

 R 1.0 Word Analysis, Fluency, and Systematic Vocabulary Development

Using the Word Study Steps

1. LOOK at the word.
2. SAY the word aloud.
3. STUDY the letters in the word.

4. WRITE the word.
5. CHECK the word.
   Did you spell the word right?
   If not, go back to step 1.

A. Missing Vowels

Fill in the missing vowels to form spelling words.

1. ch ___ c ___ l ___ t ___
2. ___ gl ___ ___
3. c ___ r ___ b ___ ___
4. y ___ cht
5. p ___ ___ dl ___
6. b ___ rb ___ c ___ ___
7. g ___ ng
8. br ___ nc ___
9. b ___ ll ___ t
10. b ___ z ___ ___ r

11. pl ___ t ___ ___ ___
12. pl ___ z ___
13. s ___ mbr ___ r ___
14. cr ___ ___ s ___
15. ___ pr ___ c ___ t
16. c ___ n ___ ___
17. d ___ n ___ m
18. p ___ j ___ m ___ s
19. b ___ lc ___ ny
20. p ___ zz ___

B. Make a Puzzle

Make up a puzzle of your own using the space on this page. Give it to someone else to solve. Be sure to include at least five spelling words in your puzzle.

LC 1.5 Spell frequently misspelled words correctly (e.g., *their, they're, there*).

© Macmillan/McGraw-Hill

Name _____

A. Proofreading

There are five spelling mistakes in the paragraph below. Circle the misspelled words. Write the words correctly on the lines below.

Last night I had the strangest dream. I was walking my poodal and all of a sudden a large gonga in the center of the town plasa began to ring, alerting everyone that the volcano was preparing to erupt. I ran home, packed my paagamuz, and headed out of town. I was scared that if I stuck around I would wind up like barbacue from the lava of the volcano.

1. _____   2. _____   3. _____

4. _____   5. _____

B. Writing Activity

Have you ever had a really silly dream? Write a short story about it. Use at least five spelling words.

_____

_____

_____

_____

_____

_____

_____

_____

_____

_____

_____

_____

LC 1.5 Spell frequently misspelled words correctly
(e.g., *their*, *they're*, *there*).

The Dog of Pompeii • Grade 6/Unit 5   **273**

Name _____

A **compound sentence** is made up of two sentences that are combined with a comma and a conjunction, such as *and*, *but*, and *or*. (I enjoy swimming. I also enjoy hiking. *I enjoy swimming, and I also enjoy hiking.*) If the parts of a compound sentence are not joined by a comma and a conjunction, use a semicolon (Jim likes basketball. His brother does not. *Jim likes basketball; his brother does not.*)

A **complex sentence** is made up of one independent clause and one or more dependent clauses. Example: *As I walked home after school, I noticed dark storm clouds forming in the sky.*

A **compound-complex sentence** is made up of two independent clauses and one or more dependent clauses. Example: *While we all held our breath, Jen scored the winning goal, and we won the state championship.*

A. Combine the following sentences to form compound sentences.

1. Jennifer loves to take long walks in the park. Her brother Jason would rather stay home. _____

   _____

2. Michael really enjoys skiing. He also likes to snowboard. _____

   _____

B. Underline the independent clauses, and circle the dependent clauses in the following sentences.

3. After we finished the game, I walked home.

4. Although he was tired, Joe did well on the test.

LC 1.1 Use simple, compound, and compound-complex sentences; use effective coordination and subordination of ideas to express complete thoughts.

Name _____

A **compound sentence** is two sentences that are combined with a comma and a conjunction, such as *and*, *but*, and *or*. If the parts of a compound sentence are not joined by a comma and a conjunction, use a semicolon.

A **complex sentence** is made up of one independent clause and one or more dependent clauses.

A **compound-complex sentence** is made up of two independent clauses and one or more dependent clauses.

Proofread this passage. Then combine some of the shorter sentences to create compound, complex, and compound-complex sentences.

Tendai grew up in a large house in south-central Africa. Not only did he live with his parents, brothers and sisters. His grandparents, several aunts, uncles, and cousins lived there, too! Even though many people lived in the house. it never seemed crowded. Elders took special care of the children. Children were considerate of their elders. Tendai especially loved walking to and from school with his siblings and cousins. Some days they had races. on other days they stopped by the shops for a soda.

_____
_____
_____
_____
_____
_____
_____
_____
_____
_____

© Macmillan/McGraw-Hill

LC 1.1 Use simple, compound, and compound-complex sentences; use effective coordination and subordination of ideas to express complete thoughts.

The Dog of Pompeii • **Grade 6/Unit 5** **275**

Excerpt from "Robert's Day"
by Christina Reilly

The old man sat alone eating his ice cream. He looked up through the rotunda of Quincy Market and smiled at the old signs on the wall above the balcony. He could barely walk, but he could still read those signs. He remembered when such signs were all over the city, advertising products like Cream Margarine. Margarine used to come without the color; the color was sold in a separate package, and you mixed it yourself. Robert's father refused to mix the color in. He said, "If it ain't butter, why make it look like it?" His father was pretty sure. Today, as he did every day, Robert Finch came here to eat lunch and watch people in the rotunda.

Finishing the ice cream, he stood up slowly and, using his cane to open the door, stepped out into the light summer drizzle. Usually, he would stay at Quincy Market, just people-watching, but today was special. Walking back to his apartment in the West End, he whistled.

1. **Read** the excerpt from "Robert's Day" at the top of the page.

2. **Think:** What is the **argument** the author is trying to make?
   What is the **evidence** she used to support her argument?

3. **Write** 4–6 sentences for the following prompt. Use evidence from "Robert's Day":

   Prompt: I can tell that Robert is happy because. . .

_____
_____
_____
_____
_____
_____
_____
_____
_____

© Macmillan/McGraw-Hill

Name _____

Some words in English have **Latin roots**. When you know
particular roots, you can often figure out the meaning of a word.
Roots do not normally stand on their own, so they are often in the
middle of a word, surrounded by prefixes and/or suffixes.

**Underline the Latin root of each word. Use the word in a
sentence that makes the meaning clear. Use a dictionary
if you need to.**

1. project _____

_____

2. biography _____

_____

3. bookmobile _____

_____

4. microscope _____

_____

5. tractor _____

_____

6. manuscript _____

_____

7. flexible _____

_____

8. periscope _____

_____

Name _____

Use the vocabulary words below to complete the sentences.

affected	despite	region
trigger	undertook	

1. The Gonzales family decided to go camping _____ the looming rain clouds.

2. Caroline _____ the outcome of the game when she made the goal in the last two seconds.

3. Jezzie _____ the job of caring for the classroom plants over summer vacation.

4. The savannah _____ of Africa is filled with animals of all kinds, all of which are dependent on the grasses that grow here.

5. People who understand their own personalities really well can anticipate

   the events that might _____ a bad mood or crankiness, and avoid them.

Now write your own sentence for each vocabulary word above.

6. _____

7. _____

8. _____

9. _____

10. _____

 R 1.0 Word Analysis, Fluency, and Systematic Vocabulary Development

Name _____

An event or action that makes something happen is a **cause**. What happens as a result of that event or action is the **effect**. Authors often use signal words and phrases such as *as a result*, *so*, *therefore*, *because*, *due to*, and *then* to identify causes and effects.

Read the following passage. Underline the signal words or phrases that show the relationships between events. Then write the cause and effect of each situation on the lines that follow.

The sudden release of energy underneath the surface of Earth can result in an earthquake. An earthquake is when two or more tectonic plates either ram into each other or get stuck together and put a strain on the ground above. Seismic waves are then released in Earth's crust, causing the surface to shake or vibrate, sometimes violently.

When a serious earthquake occurs, entire sections of the ground can be displaced. Tsunamis can result from such situations. After a tsunami, there can be considerable destruction of property or even a loss of life in the affected regions.

1. cause _____

   _____

   effect _____

2. cause _____

   effect _____

3. cause _____

   effect _____

4. cause _____

   effect _____

5. cause _____

   effect _____

CA **R 2.0** Reading Comprehension (Focus on Informational Materials).

Name _____

As you read *The Big One*, fill in the Cause and Effect Chart.

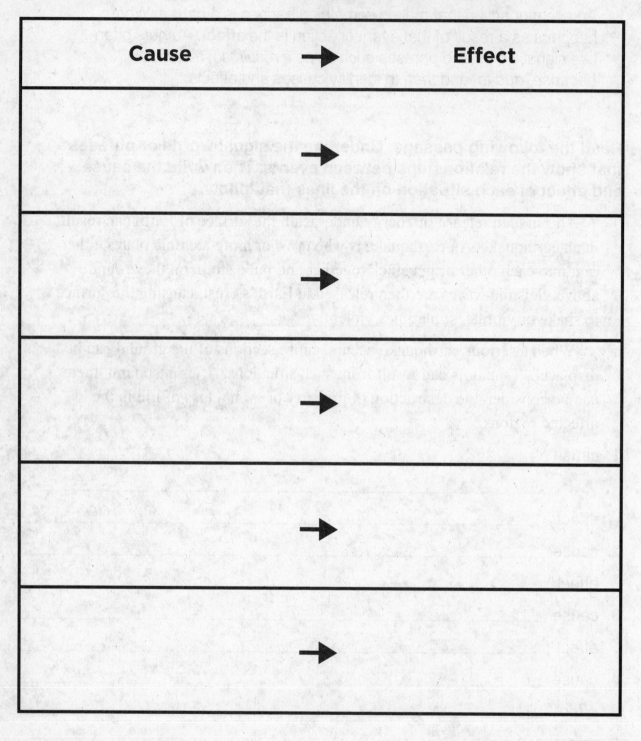

Cause	➡	Effect
	➡	
	➡	
	➡	
	➡	
	➡	

How does the information you wrote in the Cause and Effect Chart help you
better understand *The Big One*?

CA **R 2.0** Reading Comprehension (Focus on Informational Materials)

Name _____

As I read, I will pay attention to phrasing.

	The Bureau of Engraving and Printing (BEP) prints all paper
10	money in the United States. The BEP was founded in 1862 during the
22	Civil War. Until that time, the federal government did not issue paper
34	money. Today it prints trillions of dollars in bills every year. Most of
47	the money that the BEP prints will replace bills that are worn or torn.
61	Paper money is very strong. But even so, dollar bills wear out in two
75	years. Others last longer, depending on their amount. The continuous
85	folding and handling of money wears the bills out.
94	The BEP prints bills in the following denominations: $1, $5, $10,
102	$20, $50, and $100. Bills are printed at different plants. One is in
112	Washington, D.C., and the other is in Fort Worth, Texas. Every day
124	the two plants turn out about 37 million bills with a value of almost
137	$700 million!
138	The new $20 bill contains many new security features. It has been
149	carefully designed to prevent counterfeiters from making fake money.
158	The BEP takes special care in printing bills. The bills need to last
171	as long as possible. The BEP uses special paper and inks to make
184	the bills strong. The paper and ink are also hard for outsiders to copy.
198	All through history, criminals have printed counterfeit money. 206

Comprehension Check

1. Summarize the duties of the BEP. **Summarize**

2. Why do you think paper bills feel different from regular paper? **Make Inferences**

	Words Read	–	Number of Errors	=	Words Correct Score
First Read		–		=	
Second Read		–		=	

© Macmillan/McGraw-Hill

R 1.1 Read aloud narrative and expository text fluently and accurately and with appropriate pacing, intonation, and expression.

A **dictionary** lists definitions of words. It also provides the syllable division, the pronunciation, and the parts of speech. Look at this entry:

> **vol•ca•no** (vŏl-cānō) *n.* **1.** A vent in Earth's crust through which molten lava and gases are ejected. **2.** A mountain formed by the molten lava ejected through a vent in Earth's crust.

A **thesaurus** lists synonyms and antonyms of a word. It also lists the different parts of speech. Look at this entry:

Example: active

NOUN
voice   in grammar: active voice

ADJECTIVE
1. energetic   vigorous, strenuous, forceful
2. moving   stirring, in motion
3. lively   animated, spirited, bubbly

ANTONYMS: inactive, inert, non-moving

Use the sample entries to answer the questions.

1. What part of speech is the word *volcano*? _____

2. What two parts of speech can the word *active* be used as?

_____

_____

3. Name a synonym for the word *active* as an adjective.

_____

_____

4. When speaking of the volcanoes that form the Hawaiian Islands, on which many people live, which definition best describes how *volcano* is used?

_____

_____

© Macmillan/McGraw-Hill

 R 2.0 Reading Comprehension (Focus on Informational Materials).

Name _____

Cause/Effect Writing Frame

**A. Summarize *The Big One*.
Use the Cause/Effect Writing Frame below.**

The city of San Francisco was destroyed on April 18, 1906. The **cause** of this was _____
_____.

As a result of the quakes, _____
_____
_____.

Another disastrous **effect** of the quakes was _____
_____.

In addition, _____
_____
_____.

San Franciscans did not give up. **Because** their city needed help, they _____
_____
_____.

As a result, in three years _____
_____.

**B. Rewrite the completed summary on another sheet of paper. Keep it as
a model for writing a summary of an article or selection using this text
structure.**

 R 2.0 Reading Comprehension

© Macmillan/McGraw-Hill

When you read a paragraph, you may come across unfamiliar words. Use **context clues** within the paragraph to help you understand these words.

Read the paragraph and then follow the directions that follow.

The day the volcano erupted won't soon be forgotten. The <u>destruction</u> was profound, with hundreds of homes covered in ash and completely ruined. No one expected such an <u>incident</u> to take place here. I suppose we should have known an event like this was coming; we do live on the foothills of an active volcano, after all, But even the stories we'd heard of eruptions didn't prepare us for how <u>explosive</u> it would be. It wasn't as though lava quietly dribbled down the mountain. It came shooting out of the top, as though a bomb went off in there. But what's truly amazing is how the entire island banded together to rebuild. That was no easy <u>feat</u>. And we couldn't have achieved it had we not all worked together to pitch in.

1. Circle the context clues that help you understand the word *destruction*, and then write a definition of the word. _____

   _____

2. Circle the context clues that help you understand the word *incident*, and then write a definition of the word. _____

3. Circle the context clues that help you understand the word *explosive*, and then write a definition of the word. _____

   _____

4. Circle the context clues that help you understand the word *feat*, and then write a definition of the word. _____

5. Now write a sentence of your own using at least two of the underlined words.

   _____

   _____

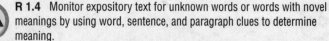

R 1.4 Monitor expository text for unknown words or words with novel meanings by using word, sentence, and paragraph clues to determine meaning.

Name _____

Using the Word Study Steps

1. LOOK at the word.
2. SAY the word aloud.
3. STUDY the letters in the word.

4. WRITE the word.
5. CHECK the word.
   Did you spell the word right?
   If not, go back to step 1.

A. Missing Letters

Fill in the missing letters to form spelling words.

1. pre_____tion
2. struc_____
3. _____dit
4. fac_____
5. educ_____
6. _____ject
7. _____ible
8. dest_____tion
9. _____dio
10. re_____tion
11. ob_____tion
12. ins_____
13. bene_____
14. sec_____
15. de_____ed
16. i_____duce
17. in_____ible
18. re_____e
19. dict_____ary
20. aud_____ce

B. Make a Puzzle

Make up a puzzle of your own using the space on this page. Give it to someone else to solve. Be sure to include at least five spelling words in your puzzle.

© Macmillan/McGraw-Hill

CA LC 1.5 Spell frequently misspelled words correctly (e.g., *their, they're, there*).

The Big One • **Grade 6/Unit 5** **285**

A. Proofreading

There are five spelling mistakes in the paragraph below. Circle the misspelled words. Write the words correctly on the line below.

     The hurricane that struck the town of Short Falls left a path of distruction. The local television station hosted an evening to benefit those who had lost so much to the natural disaster. The audiance of the program heard many incredable stories that night. There was no objection to a repeat performance of the educashon program.

1. _____ 2. _____ 3. _____

4. _____ 5. _____

B. Writing Activity

Did your town or neighborhood ever come together for a specific cause? Write a paragraph describing this event. Use five spelling words.

_____

_____

_____

_____

_____

_____

_____

_____

_____

_____

_____

© Macmillan/McGraw-Hill

 LC 1.5 Spell frequently misspelled words correctly (e.g., *their, they're, there*).

Name _____

- The **comparative** form of an adjective compares two nouns.
- The **superlative** form compares more than two nouns.
- Add -*er* or -*est* to most one-syllable and some two-syllable adjectives to form the comparative and superlative.
- For adjectives ending in *e*, drop the *e* before adding -*er* or -*est*.
- For adjectives ending in a consonant and *y*, change *y* to *i* and add -*er* and -*est*.
- For one-syllable adjectives that have a single vowel before a final consonant, double the final consonant before adding -*er* or -*est*.

Complete each sentence with the correct comparative or superlative form of the adjective in parentheses. On the line after the sentence, write the correct form of another adjective that also makes sense in the sentence.

1. Theo is the (young) _____ member of the group.

_____

2. It was the (busy) _____ group he had ever joined.

_____

3. Their leader was the (happy) _____ woman Theo knew.

_____

4. She was also the (wise) _____ person he had ever met.

_____

5. It was (hot) _____ today than it was yesterday.

_____

6. This building is (tall) _____ than that one.

_____

© Macmillan/McGraw-Hill

- The **comparative** form of an adjective compares two nouns.
- The **superlative** form compares more than two nouns.

Proofread the point-of-view essay below for any errors in the use of comparative and superlative adjectives, punctuation, or capitalization.

i have been asked to comment on the fast most economical way our club can bring aid to hungry children. we could collect nonperishable food. Collecting, packing, and shipping the food would be difficult, however? Who would distribute it! How would the children receive it.

A smartest solution I believe is to collect money. Money is easy to collect easy to send overseas and easy for relief agencies, like the red cross, to put to good use. With money, agencies can buy food medicine or clothing--- whatever is needed. If I had to choose between sending food or sending money money is the smartest choice.

_____

_____

_____

_____

_____

_____

_____

_____

_____

_____

_____

_____

 LC 1.0 Written and Oral English Language Conventions

Writing Rubric

	4 Excellent	3 Good	2 Fair	1 Unsatisfactory
	Ideas and Content/Genre	Ideas and Content/Genre	Ideas and Content/Genre	Ideas and Content/Genre
	Organization and Focus	Organization and Focus	Organization and Focus	Organization and Focus
	Sentence Structure/Fluency	Sentence Structure/Fluency	Sentence Structure/Fluency	Sentence Structure/Fluency
	Conventions	Conventions	Conventions	Conventions
	Word Choice	Word Choice	Word Choice	Word Choice
	Voice	Voice	Voice	Voice
	Presentation	Presentation	Presentation	Presentation

© Macmillan/McGraw-Hill

Some words in the English language have **Greek roots.** When you know the meaning of the Greek roots, you can figure out meanings of new words. Roots do not normally stand on their own. They can be in the middle of a word or surrounded by prefixes and/or suffixes. Sometimes the prefixes and the suffixes are also from Greek roots.

Underline the Greek root or roots of each word. Then write the meaning of the word on the line following it. Use a dictionary to help.

1. autograph _____

2. chronological _____

3. astronomy _____

   _____

4. photography _____

   _____

5. ecological _____

   _____

6. biology _____

7. automobile _____

8. telegraph _____

   _____

R 1.0 Word Analysis, Fluency, and Systematic Vocabulary Development

© Macmillan/McGraw-Hill

Use the clues below to complete the crossword.

affects   mass   collision   transported
aerial   established   methods   century

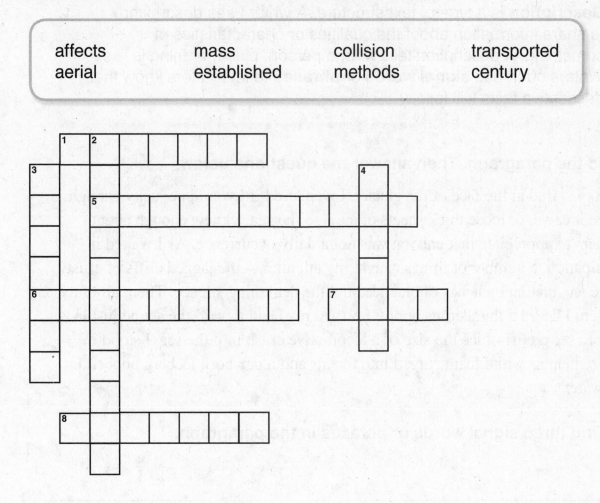

Across

1. organized ways of doing things
5. moved from one place to another
6. what happens when two moving things hit each other
7. a large mound of material
8. one hundred years in a row

Down

2. started or set up
3. has an influence on
4. a view of things from the air

Name _____

> **Description** is a type of text structure. A writer uses description to share information about the qualities or characteristics of something. A description tells what a person, place, or thing is like. Writers often use **signal words** or **phrases** to let readers know that descriptive facts will follow.

Read the paragraph. Then answer the questions below.

As I stared at the face of the glacier, I wondered if I would be lucky enough to see it calve, or loose thick sheets of ice into the sea. I knew enough about glaciers to appreciate that calving was not a daily occurrence. As I waited in anticipation, a number of things caught my attention—the jagged cliffs of crusty white ice, brilliant patches of blue ice, and the deafening silence. Then, all of a sudden, I heard a thunderous boom. I turned my head toward the sound just in time to see a cliff of ice the size of a locomotive crash into the sea. I stood in amazement as white foam surged into the air and a newborn iceberg bobbed in the water.

A. Find three signal words or phrases in the paragraph.

1. _____

2. _____

3. _____

B. Find three descriptive facts in the paragraph.

4. _____

5. _____

6. _____

© Macmillan/McGraw-Hill

 R 2.0 Reading Comprehension (Focus on Informational Materials)

Name _____

As you read *Icebergs and Glaciers*, fill in the Description Chart.

Signal Words	Descriptive Facts

How does the Description Chart help you understand *Icebergs and Glaciers*?

As I read, I will pay attention to intonation and phrasing.

	César Chávez was one of the great labor leaders of our
11	time. Some people are driven to improve the lives of those
22	around them. César Chávez was that kind of person.
31	When Chávez was young, he and his family were
40	migrant workers. They traveled from field to field picking
49	crops. This meant the Chávez children changed schools
57	often. It also meant that the Chávez family remained poor
67	and had no permanent home.
72	César's life was filled with hardship, yet he never gave in.
83	He spent his life fighting to improve the lives of migrant
94	workers. Because of Chávez, the lives of campesinos
102	(kam-puh-SEE-nohs), or farmworkers, are much better today.
108	Césario Estrada Chávez was born on March 31, 1927,
117	near Yuma, Arizona. He was the second child of Librado
127	and Juana Chávez. César was named for his grandfather,
136	which was telling. To escape oppression by the harsh
145	government, his grandfather had fled Mexico in the 1880s.
154	He claimed land in Arizona and started a farm. César was
165	influenced by his grandfather's love of farming and his desire
175	for a better life. 179

Comprehension Check

1. What hardships did the Chávez family experience? **Summarize**

2. What is César Chávez famous for doing? **Main Ideas and Details**

© Macmillan/McGraw-Hill

	Words Read	–	Number of Errors	=	Words Correct Score
First Read		–		=	
Second Read		–		=	

 R 1.1 Read aloud narrative and expository text fluently and accurately and with appropriate pacing, intonation, and expression.

Name _____

> **Personification** is a type of figurative language in which the poet gives an object or an idea human actions or a human personality. Example: The moon winked at the earth below.
>
> **Rhyme** is the use of words that end in the same sound or in very similar sounds.
> Example: Jack and *Jill*
>   Went up the *hill*
>
> **Repetition** involves saying a word or phrase several times for rhythmic effect and emphasis.
> Example: Merrily, merrily, merrily, merrily,
>   Life is but a dream.

A. Circle the pair of words that rhyme.

1. a. twist/twice   b. chord/board   c. portion/piece

2. a. pollution/solution   b. fragrant/fresh   c. thought/enough

B. Read each personification and answer the questions.

The snow whispered as it drifted by my window.

3. Why is this an example of personification?

_____

The waves beckoned to the surfers on the beach.

4. Why is this an example of personification?

_____

C. Write a short poem about a melting iceberg that includes repetition. If possible, include examples of personification and rhyme.

_____

_____

CA R 3.7 Explain the effects of common literary devices (e.g., symbolism, imagery, metaphor) in a variety of fictional and nonfictional texts.

Icebergs and Glaciers   **295**
Grade 6/Unit 5

Name _____

Dictionaries provide readers with the histories of words as well as their meanings. The **word's origin** usually follows the pronunciation key and the identification of its part of speech. If you don't understand the abbreviations in the entry, check the front of the dictionary for a guide to the abbreviations. Some common ones are ME for Middle English, OE for Old English, F for French, L for Latin, and Gk for Greek.

Example: collide (kə 'lid) *v* [L collidere, from *com-+laedere* to injure by striking] 1. to come together with forceful impact

A. Use a dictionary to find the origins of the words below. Record the earliest origin listed in the dictionary.

1. barber _____

2. collage _____

3. foreign _____

4. tentacle _____

5. guest _____

B. Use each of the words above in a sentence. Include the word of origin in the sentence as a context clue.

6. _____

_____

7. _____

_____

8. _____

_____

9. _____

_____

10. _____

_____

CA R 1.0 Word Analysis, Fluency, and Systematic Vocabulary Development

© Macmillan/McGraw-Hill

Name _____

Using the Word Study Steps

1. LOOK at the word.

2. SAY the word aloud.

3. STUDY the letters in the word.

4. WRITE the word.

5. CHECK the word.
Did you spell the word right?
If not, go back to step 1.

Crossword Puzzle

Use the clues to complete the puzzle.

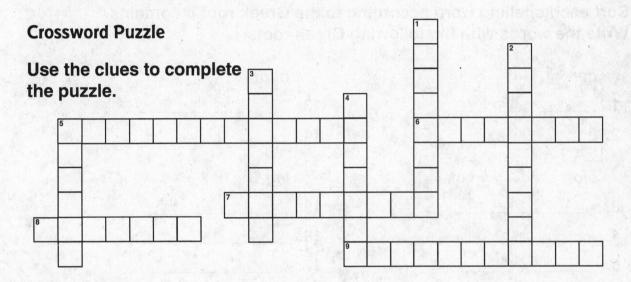

DOWN

1. I enjoyed the orchestra's beatiful rendition of the _____.

2. At the science museum I liked the _____ exhibit.

3. My grandmother has a _____ cough.

4. The fire _____ contains water to fight fires.

5. The photographer took _____ photos while skydiving.

ACROSS

5. When I get older I will write my _____.

6. Water is composed of _____ and oxygen.

7. I can't wait to read the new _____ of my favorite singer.

8. I ordered new shoes from a sneaker _____.

9. My doctor used a _____ to take my temperature.

 R 1.0 Word Analysis, Fluency, and
Systematic Vocabulary Development.

Icebergs and Glaciers
Grade 6/Unit 5
297

© Macmillan/McGraw-Hill

aerial	aerospace	autobiography	paragraph	biography
biology	diagram	microwave	hydrant	grammar
catalog	thermometer	microscope	microphone	chronic
programs	hydrogen	dialogue	thermal	symphony

**Sort each spelling word according to the Greek root it contains.
Write the words with the following Greek roots:**

aer

1. _____
2. _____

bio

3. _____
4. _____
5. _____

chron

6. _____

gram

7. _____
8. _____
9. _____

graph

10. _____
11. _____
12. _____

hydr

13. _____
14. _____

log

15. _____
16. _____
17. _____

micro

18. _____
19. _____
20. _____

phon

21. _____
22. _____

scope

23. _____

© Macmillan/McGraw-Hill

R 1.0 Word Analysis, Fluency, and
Systematic Vocabulary Development

> • Never use *more* or *most* with the *-er* or *-est* form of an
>   adjective.

On the line provided, write the comparative or superlative adjective that correctly completes each sentence.

1. Hannah has the (most amazing, amazingest) collection of bells.

   _____

2. She claims to choose only the (most pretty, prettiest) bells.

   _____

3. I've noticed that the sound of Hannah's bells is (more pleasing, pleasinger) than most.

   _____

4. The steel bell sounds (worse, worst) than the glass bell.

   _____

5. Hannah's collection of bells is the (largest, most large) I've ever seen.

   _____

6. The sound of this bell is (more deep, deeper) than the sound of that one.

   _____

7. This little bell has the (good, best) sound of all.

   _____

8. When we ring Hannah's bells all at once, the house is the (most noisy, noisiest) it's ever been.

   _____

9. Diana is (more eager, eagerer) than Tasha to start a bell collection.

   _____

10. Diana probably will get her first bell (more soon, sooner) than Tasha.

   _____

Name _____

- For most adjectives with two or more syllables, use *more* to form the comparative.
- For most adjectives with two or more syllables, use *most* to form the superlative.

Mechanics

- Never use *more* or *most* with the *-er* or *-est* form of an adjective.
- Each line of a poem usually begins with a capital letter.

Put brackets [ ] around any comparative or superlative adjectives. Correct any mistakes in adjective use. Then rewrite the poems, using correct punctuation.

three wise men of Gotham
went to sea in a bowl.
If the bowl had been stronger
my song would have been longer.

my bells sing so sweetly,
most sweetly than yours.
my bells look so lovely,
the lovelier of all.

_____
_____
_____
_____
_____
_____
_____

 LC 1.0 Written and Oral English Language Conventions

© Macmillan/McGraw-Hill

Name _____

1. **Read:** Tanya thought, "This room gives me the creeps."

2. **Write** 3 sentences that describe the room Tanya is in. Write 1 sentence that shows how Tanya is reacting to the setting.

_____

_____

_____

_____

_____

_____

_____

_____

_____

_____

_____

_____

_____

_____

_____

_____

_____

_____

You add the suffix *-ive* to a verb to change it to an adjective. It shows a state of being. The vowel in the suffix is short.

Example: attract + *ive* = attractive

You add the suffix *-age* to a verb to change it to a noun. It shows an action, a state, a number, or the cost of something. Sometimes you drop the last **e**. The vowel in this suffix is short.

Examples: post + *age* = postage
store + *age* = storage

You add the suffix *-ize* to a noun to make it a verb. The vowel in this suffix follows the VCe pattern. It has a long *i* sound.

Example: civil + *ize* = civilize

A. Read the sentences. Underline the words that follow the patterns described above.

1. When I went scuba diving, I saw the wreckage of a ship.

2. The guide on the whale-watching tour told us about the whale's parentage.

3. The beauty of the water made its strength seem deceptive.

4. The teacher asked us to verbalize the answers to his questions as he tape-recorded us.

5. We hope to formalize the agreement between the school and the state.

6. The work we have done is impressive.

B. Use some of the words above or others that have suffixes to make up sentences of your own. Underline the word with the suffix.

7. _____

_____

8. _____

_____

 R 1.0 Word Analysis, Fluency, and Systematic Vocabulary Development

Name _____

A. Write the vocabulary word that completes each sentence.

formations	wreckage	intact	severed
interior	hovering	emerged	clockwise

1. Oceanographers study the _____ of ships that have been underwater for many years.

2. Coral _____ often make up reefs where underwater life is abundant.

3. Finding an _____ ship or airplane is rare, because most have sunk to the ocean floor.

4. Fish and divers alike are _____ above the ocean floor in the water.

5. Seeing the _____, or inside, of the *Titanic* is amazing!

B. Write sentences using these vocabulary words: *emerged*, *severed*, *clockwise*. Write about an experience with the ocean or with creatures that live in water.

6. _____

_____

7. _____

_____

8. _____

_____

A. Read the passage. Then record three facts and three opinions presented in it.

Oceanography is the most interesting branch of science. Oceanographers go whale watching and even swim with sharks. Doing that must be really scary. They study all the animals in the ocean. Oceanographers also scuba dive. They learn to use computers that tell them about water. They even study weather. I think that being an oceanographer would be the best job in the world!

Facts:

- _____
- _____
- _____

Opinions:

- _____
- _____
- _____

B. What is, in your opinion, the best job in the world? Write a paragraph that contains facts and opinions to answer the question.

_____

_____

_____

_____

_____

_____

_____

© Macmillan/McGraw-Hill

 R 2.0 Reading Comprehension (Focus on Informational Materials)

As you read *Exploring the Titanic*, fill in the Fact and Opinion Chart.

Fact	Opinion

How does the information you wrote in this Fact and Opinion Chart help you evalute *Exploring the Titanic*?

As I read, I will pay attention to phrasing.

	Jacques Cousteau did not begin his life near the sea. He was
12	born in 1910 in France. His hometown of St.-André-de-Cubzac
20	[sant on-DRAY duh koob-ZOK] is set along a river.
25	Jacques was often sick as a boy, so he did not spend as
38	much time outside as his adventurous spirit would have liked.
48	Most of his adventures came from his reading. Jacques loved
58	books about pirates, pearl divers, and distant seas.
66	Jacques had another habit during childhood. He loved
74	inventions and toying with all kinds of machinery. He saved
84	his allowance to buy one of the first movie cameras sold in
96	France. He taught himself to take it apart and put it back
108	together. When he was 13, he used the camera to shoot his
119	first film.
121	When he was a young man, Cousteau joined the navy.
131	As he traveled around the world, he became more and more
142	interested in the sea. One bright weekend morning in 1936,
151	the young sailor waded into the waters of the Mediterranean
161	Sea. 162

Comprehension Check

1. What may have influenced Jacques's decision to join the navy? **Draw Conclusions**

2. How do you know that Jacques was good at understanding machinery? **Draw Conclusions**

	Words Read	–	Number of Errors	=	Words Correct Score
First Read		–		=	
Second Read		–		=	

 R 1.1 Read aloud narrative and expository text fluently and accurately and with appropriate pacing, intonation, and expression.

A tall tale features a larger-than-life hero who solves a problem in a funny or outrageous way. It includes exaggerated details.

Hyperbole is the use of exaggeration for emphasis.

Dialogue is a conversation between two or more characters. It is usually set off by quotation marks.

Common American heroes of tall tales include Johnny Appleseed, Paul Bunyan and Babe the Blue Ox, Pecos Bill and Widow Maker, and Slue-Foot Sue. All of their tales include elements of exaggeration, or hyperbole. For example, Pecos Bill was raised by coyotes, so he had a special relationship with wild animals. He first chose to ride a lion instead of a horse. When he decided on a horse to ride, he chose one that no one else would dare go near because it was so wild. Paul Bunyan was an enormous man who, with the help of his blue ox, felled many trees. He was a woodsman.

Choose one of these American heroes of tall tales and write a tall tale yourself. Be sure to include dialogue and hyperbole.

_____

_____

_____

_____

_____

_____

_____

_____

_____

Words consist of a variety of parts: prefixes, base words, suffixes, and inflectional endings. **Suffixes** are the parts that are added at the end of words. Suffixes change the meanings and the functions of words.

Example: When I went deep-sea diving, I saw the *wreckage* of a sunken ship.

The suffix *-age* is added to the base word *wreck*. The suffix means "state of being," so the word means "something that has been wrecked." You can use your knowledge of suffixes to determine word meanings.

Write the new word formed by adding the suffixes below to the base word. Then write what the new word means.

1. active + ity = _____

2. swim + er = _____

3. place + ment = _____

4. trace + able = _____

5. hope + ful = _____

6. captive + ity = _____

7. drive + er = _____

8. state + ment = _____

9. afford + able = _____

10. cheer + ful = _____

 R 1.0 Word Analysis, Fluency, and Systematic Vocabulary Development

© Macmillan/McGraw-Hill

Name _____

Using the Word Study Steps

1. **LOOK** at the word.
2. **SAY** the word aloud.
3. **STUDY** the letters in the word.
4. **WRITE** the word.
5. **CHECK** the word. Did you spell the word right? If not, go back to step 1.

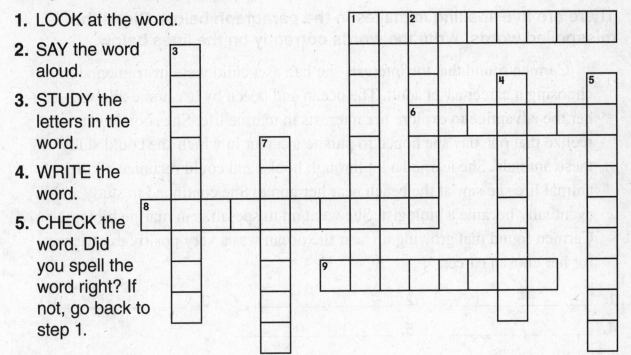

Crossword Puzzle

Use the clues to complete the puzzle.

ACROSS

1. My grandfather likes to _____ ideas he finds important.

6. We put the extra furniture into _____.

8. The flowers and the artwork helped to make the room more _____.

9. Min was upset about the _____ feedback on her art project.

DOWN

1. Fireworks are highly _____.

2. The explorers were looking for a new _____ to Asia.

3. Preparing for the exam proved to be a huge _____.

4. I joined the art club to explore my _____ talents.

5. The class was very _____ when planning the surprise party.

7. On my last visit to the planetarium, I began to _____ how fascinating the solar system is.

 LC 1.5 Spell frequently misspelled words correctly (e.g., *their, they're, there*).

A. Proofreading Activity

There are five spelling mistakes in the paragraph below. Circle the misspelled words. Write the words correctly on the lines below.

Carmen found that the interests she had as a child were instrumental in choosing a career as an adult. The ocean and beach by her home allowed her the advantige to explore her interests in marine life. She soon began to reelize that one day she hoped to pursue a career in which she could study these animals. She learned a lot through books and could reconize all the animal life she saw at the beach near her home. She continued to study and eventually became a biologist. She went on to spesalize in marine biology. Carmen found that growing up near the ocean was a very positiv experience for her chosen career.

1. _____   2. _____   3. _____

4. _____   5. _____

B. Writing Activity

What do you like to do more than anything? Write a story about how you might take this passion and turn it into a career. Use five spelling words.

_____

_____

_____

_____

_____

_____

_____

_____

© Macmillan/McGraw-Hill

 LC 1.5 Spell frequently misspelled words correctly (e.g., *their, they're, there*).

A **verb phrase** is made up of a main verb and a helping verb. The **tense** of the helping verb tells us *when* an action happened or will happen.

Tense	When?	Example
Present perfect	in the past; the exact time is not important	I **have played** soccer.
Past perfect	in the past, before another event took place	I **had played soccer** before I learned to play basketball.
Future perfect	in the future, before another event happens	I **will have finished** the soccer season by November.

A. Name the tense of the following verbs.

1. will have walked _____

2. have worked _____

3. will have tried _____

4. have waited _____

5. had laughed _____

B. For each sentence, change the verb to the tense shown in parentheses. Write the new sentence below.

6. We walk to the museum. (present perfect)

_____

7. We listen to a story. (past perfect)

_____

8. We enter the theater. (future perfect)

_____

LC 1.2 Identify and properly use indefinite pronouns and present perfect, past perfect, and future perfect verb tenses; ensure that verbs agree with compound subjects.

Exploring the Titanic
Grade 6/Unit 5   **311**

Name _____

Practice

Grammar:
Present Perfect,
Past Perfect, and
Future Perfect Verbs

- Use the **present perfect** tense to say that an action happened sometime in the past. The exact time is not important.

  Example: I **have watched** the show many times.

- Use the **past perfect** tense to say that something happened before another action in the past.

  Example: I **had watched** the show before I went to bed.

- Use the **future perfect** tense to show that something will happen before another action in the future.

  Example: I **will have finished** my homework by bedtime.

Proofread this passage. Then rewrite the passage using the correct verb tense. Correct any mistakes in capitalization or punctuation.

last night i dreamed that my family had moved to the North Pole i have dreamed about the North Pole before. In last night's dream, my family had discover an empty house on an iceberg. by the end of my dream, we had drift to the middle of the ocean. The iceberg had start to shrinked. My sister and I had make a boat. I told her, "By the time the iceberg melts, we will have sail away." When I woke up, I was freezing. I had wrap myself in my blanket.

_____

_____

_____

_____

_____

_____

_____

_____

© Macmillan/McGraw-Hill

LC 1.2 Identify and properly use indefinite pronouns and present perfect, past perfect, and future perfect verb tenses; ensure that verbs agree with compound subjects.

"An Open Window"
by Emily Phillips

Cory walked into his house and slammed the door behind him. He skulked through the house to his room. Before he could slam the door, a slender, finger-nailed hand caught it.

"Where were you?" his mother asked.

"I was out," Cory replied calmly.

"You are fourteen and you should not be out so late," his mother growled softly. "And you could at least look sorry."

"Mom, it's ten o'clock. Why do you make such a big deal?" Cory grumbled. "I was out with Zach."

His mother hesitated. While she was waiting and afraid, time had passed so slowly, and she had thought it was later. "Well, I don't like Zach. He's a real punk."

1. Read "An Open Window" at the top of the page.

2. Think: Why was Cory's mom angry?
What is the **evidence** the author used to show she was mad?

3. Write 4–6 sentences for the following prompt. Use **evidence** from the story: Why was Cory's mom angry?

_____

_____

_____

_____

_____

_____

_____

The suffixes **-able** and **-ible** both mean "able or likely." You decide which spelling you will use based on whether you are attaching the suffix to a base word, such as *remark* (remark**able**) or a word root, such as *poss* (poss**ible**).

You will have to decide whether to drop the silent *e* at the end of a word when you add *-able*. Look at these two examples: *manageable* and *excusable*. When the base word ends in a soft /g/ or /c/ sound, you keep the silent *e* when you add *-able*.

Read the word parts below. Add the correct suffix, either *-able* or *-ible*. Then use each word in a sentence of your own.

1. imposs _____ _____

_____

2. reverse _____ _____

_____

3. love _____ _____

_____

4. aud _____ _____

_____

5. compat _____ _____

_____

6. horr _____ _____

_____

7. compare _____ _____

_____

8. read _____ _____

_____

© Macmillan/McGraw-Hill

 R 1.0 Word Analysis, Fluency, and Systematic Vocabulary Development

Name _____

A. Use the vocabulary words below to complete the sentences.

intersection	engulf	abruptly	conscious
anxiety	cascade	procedure	souvenir

1. Marian often had the best ideas, but her _____ about public speaking kept her from running for class president.

2. I would have liked to take a _____ from the archaeological site, but it was strictly forbidden.

3. Though the task was not difficult, I had to be careful to follow the

   _____ exactly.

4. We were startled when the author _____ closed her book and left.

5. The actor was extremely well trained—always _____ of the audience's reaction to his performance.

6. The papers fell in a _____ from the top of the shelf.

7. I was taught to look both ways when crossing an _____.

8. The huge wave was about to _____ the tiny islands in the sea.

B. Choose two of the vocabulary words in the box above and write a sentence for each.

9. _____

   _____

10. _____

   _____

   _____

© Macmillan/McGraw-Hill

Read the passage and answer the questions.

It was dark when I woke up. I was so cold. At first, I didn't know where I was. I started to panic. I couldn't move my arms or legs. What was happening to me? Then I remembered. I had been skiing. I had heard a really loud noise, like a freight train. When I had looked behind me, all I had seen was a wall of snow coming my way—fast!

"I must be buried in that snow," I said to myself. Talk about panic! Now I had a good reason. To make myself feel better, I thought about all the TV shows I had watched about people being rescued. I drifted in and out of consciousness.

Meanwhile, I learned later, the rescue teams were gathering, just like on TV! Several skiers were missing after the avalanche. Luckily, I had been skiing on a marked path. The rescue teams would know where to look for me. After what seemed like forever, I heard voices. I tried to scream, but the snow covering me blocked any noise. At last, I felt something touch my legs. A dog was digging me out. I had been rescued!

1. What do you know about the narrator? _____

_____

_____

_____

2. Where is the story set?

_____

3. How does the setting affect the story?

_____

_____

_____

4. What is the main conflict in the story?

_____

_____

_____

 R 2.0 Reading Comprehension (Focus on Informational Materials)

Name _____

As you read *The Summer of the Swans*, fill in the Story Map.

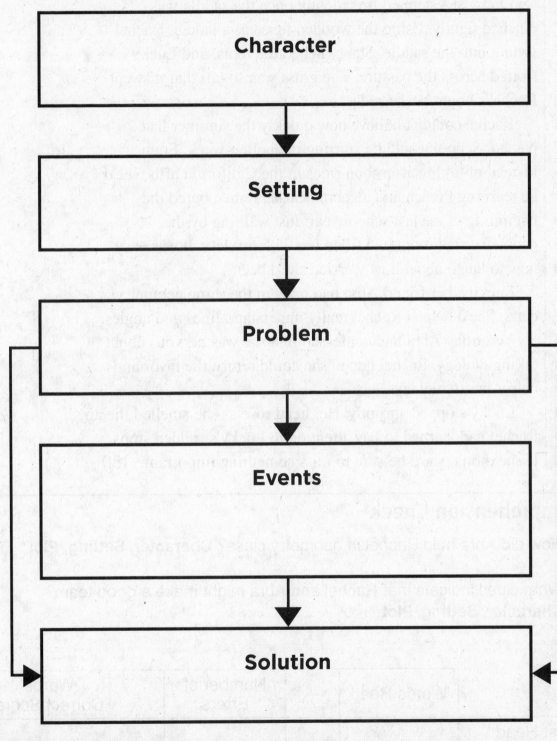

Character

Setting

Problem

Events

Solution

How does the information you wrote in this Story Map help you monitor comprehension of *The Summer of the Swans*?

Name _____

As I read, I will pay attention to intonation and phrasing.

	Lucky sidestepped impatiently once the saddle was
7	cinched tightly. Using the wooden fence as a ladder, Rachel
17	swung into the saddle. She twitched the reins, and Lucky
27	trotted across the pasture. The grass was so tall that it swept
39	Rachel's boots as she rode.
44	Rachel couldn't believe how quickly the summer had
52	passed. School would be starting in another week. Soon,
61	instead of taking afternoon rides in the California hills, she'd
71	be learning French and algebra. Rachel remembered the
79	beginning of the last school year. Just walking by the
89	geometry classroom had filled her with **anxiety**. It was easy
99	now to laugh about how worried she'd been.
107	Luckily, her friend Abra had been in the same geometry
117	class. She'd helped Rachel really understand lines and angles.
126	Yesterday Abra had confessed that she was nervous about
135	taking biology. Rachel hoped she could return the favor and
145	help Abra in biology.
149	Lucky stopped abruptly. Her head rose as she smelled the air.
160	Rachel had learned to pay attention to Lucky's sudden stops.
170	If she didn't, she'd be sure to miss something important. 180

Comprehension Check

1. How did Abra help Rachel in geometry class? **Character, Setting, Plot**

2. What clues indicate that Rachel and Abra might make a good team?
Character, Setting, Plot

	Words Read	−	Number of Errors	=	Words Correct Score
First Read		−		=	
Second Read		−		=	

R 1.1 Read aloud narrative and expository text fluently and accurately
and with appropriate pacing, **intonation**, and expression.

Name _____

Writers use **similes** and **metaphors** to compare things that are not alike.

A **simile** states that one thing is like another, using the words *like* or *as*.
Example: Lara sings like a bird.

A **metaphor** states that one thing *is* another.
Example: Lara is a songbird.

Read the passage. Answer the questions.

On a crisp winter day, I take my dog Sadie for her morning walk. We bring
along the ball. When I toss the ball, Sadie soars over the snow bank like
a white-tailed hawk. Silently, she pounces on the ground and captures her
victim. The ball is a small, defenseless creature in her grasp. With her tail
wagging, she shares her prey with me. I take it, and Sadie licks my hand.

1. Which phrase in the third sentence of the passage is an example of a
   simile? What two things are being compared? _____

   _____

   _____

2. What do you picture in your mind when you read this simile? _____

   _____

   _____

3. Which phrase in the fifth sentence of the passage is an example of a
   metaphor? What two things are being compared? _____

   _____

   _____

4. What do you picture in your mind when you read this metaphor? _____

   _____

   _____

© Macmillan/McGraw-Hill

 R 3.7 Explain the effects of common literary devices (e.g., symbolism,
imagery, metaphor) in a variety of fictional and nonfictional texts.

Multiple-meaning words have more than one definition. When you come across a multiple-meaning word, you need to determine which meaning is being used by looking at its context. These words will have various entries in the dictionary.

Consider the multiple meanings of the word *conscious*.

> **conscious** (kon shəs) *adj.*
> 1. having an awareness of one's self and one's surroundings; *The patient remained conscious after her surgery.*
> 2. fully aware of something; *I was not conscious that time was passing quickly.*
> 3. intentionally meant; *Marianne made a conscious effort not to tease her little brother.*

Each word below has more than one meaning. Use a dictionary to identify two different meanings for each word. Write two sentences—one for each meaning of the word.

1. kind

   a. _____

   b. _____

2. produce

   a. _____

   b. _____

3. proceeds

   a. _____

   b. _____

4. park

   a. _____

   b. _____

 R 1.0 Word Analysis, Fluency, and Systematic Vocabulary Development

© Macmillan/McGraw-Hill

Using the Word Study Steps

1. LOOK at the word.

2. SAY the word aloud.

3. STUDY the letters in the word.

4. WRITE the word.

5. CHECK the word.
   Did you spell the word right?
   If not, go back to step 1.

Find the Words

**Find and circle the spelling words hidden in each set of letters.
Then write them on the line.**

1. d e p e n o t i c e a b l e   _____

2. b e l i b e l i e v a b l e   _____

3. t e r r e l i a b l e i b l e   _____

4. a v a i m p o s s i b l e   _____

5. l o v a b l e p e n d a b l e   _____

6. a l w p r o v i t a v a i l a b l e   _____

7. p r e d i c t a b l e i e a b l e   _____

8. n o t i c a c c e p t a b l e   _____

9. c o n s i d e r a b l e b b l e   _____

10. p r e r e v e r e m a r k a b l e   _____

11. c o n r e v a l u a b l e i b l e   _____

12. h o r r i b c h a n g e a b l e   _____

13. r e l i a d m i r a b l e i b l e   _____

14. p r e p r o b a b l e r a t i o n   _____

15. p r e d e p e n d a b l e i b l e   _____

LC 1.5 Spell roots, suffixes, prefixes, contractions, and syllable
constructions correctly.

The Summer of the Swans   **321**
Grade 6/Unit 6

Proofreading Activity

A. There are five spelling mistakes in the paragraph below. Circle the misspelled words. Write the words correctly on the line below.

   Sidney Quinn has a remarkible collection of miniature automobiles. Sidney has been collecting cars for a considerible amount of time—nearly eighty years. He always gets excited when a new miniature car model becomes avalable. His collection has proved to be very profatabell, as some of his cars are incredibly valueable. But Sidney does not collect for the money he makes, he collects because he loves his miniature automobiles.

1. _____   2. _____   3. _____

4. _____   5. _____

Writing Activity

B. Do you have any collections? Write a paragraph describing something you collect. Use at least five spelling words.

_____

_____

_____

_____

_____

_____

_____

_____

_____

_____

 LC 1.5 Spell roots, suffixes, prefixes, contractions, and syllable constructions correctly.

Name _____

> • An **adverb** is a word that modifies a verb, an adjective, or another adverb.
> • An **adverb** can tell how, when, or where an action takes place.
> • **Adverbs** that modify adjectives and adverbs answer the questions *how?* and *to what extent?*

Read each sentence. Then put brackets [ ] around each adverb that describes an adjective or another adverb. Next, in the blank, write the adjective or adverb being modified.

1. Tameesha could sew quite well. _____

2. Her dresses were designed very classically. _____

3. "I feel completely happy when I am designing," Tameesha has said.

   _____

4. Her newest design was exceptionally fine. _____

5. Tameesha's designs are not overly dramatic. _____

6. But the dresses, shirts, and pants are always surprising.

   _____

7. Tameesha does not use very costly materials. _____

8. "Her designs are surprisingly simple," said Mr. Lewis. _____

9. Tameesha was suddenly silent when she heard that statement.

   _____

10. "I prefer to say that my clothing designs are simply classic," she

    answered. _____

- An **adverb** is a word that modifies a verb, an adjective, or another adverb.
- An **adverb** can tell how, when, or where an action takes place.
- **Adverbs** that modify adjectives and adverbs answer the questions *how?* and *to what extent?*

Mechanics

- *Good* is an adjective and is used to describe nouns.
- *Well* is an adverb that tells *how* about a verb.
- When *well* means "healthy," it is used as an adjective.

Correct any errors in the use of adverbs, and in the use of *good* and *well* in the directions below. Then rewrite the directions, correcting any errors in the use of adverbs, capitalization, or punctuation. Some sentences may be correct as is.

Tameesha quickly wrote these directions for making a simple A-line dress.

1. First, careful choose a pattern for your appropriate body type. Purchase from a well company.

2. Then buy the fabric. Don't buy very costly fabric for your first project.

3. Always read the pattern directions slow.

4. Careful cut out the pattern pieces.

_____

_____

_____

_____

_____

_____

 LC 1.0 Written and Oral English Language Conventions

Name _____

Ways to Vary Sentences:

a. Rearrange the sentence.

b. Include dialogue.

c. Change a statement to a question.

    1. Read the three "Ways to Vary Sentences" at the top of this page.

    2. Look at this example:

Florida is famous for oranges, beaches, and alligators.

      a. Oranges, beaches, and alligators are what make Florida famous.

      b. "Some day," dreamed Romie, "Some day I'll get to Florida to see beaches, oranges, and alligators."

      c. Aside from beaches, oranges, and alligators, what is Florida famous for?

    3. Read the sentence below and rewrite the sentence three times using the three "Ways to Vary Sentences".

Most of the volcanoes on the West Coast are dormant, but some are still active.

a. _____

_____

b. _____

_____

c. _____

_____

The **suffixes** -*ance*, -*ence, -ant*, and -*ent* are closely related except for the way they are spelled.

-*ance* and -*ence*	-*ant* and -*ent*
the quality of having, showing, or making what the root means	being or performing what the root means

There is no easy rule for choosing the correct spelling, but if you know the spelling of one form, then you know the spelling of the other form.

Example: resistant, resistance   present, presence

Read each sentence below and fill in the correct suffixes. Use a dictionary to help.

1. My teacher takes attend_____ every morning. My sister is

   going to have only one bridal attend_____ in her wedding.

2. A private detective must be observ_____ to do his job well. The

   stores will be closed tomorrow in observ_____ of the holiday.

3. What is the differ_____ between bluish green and greenish blue?

   How are the twins differ_____ from each other?

4. The crowd responded with great exuber_____ at the town fair.

   Some people were so exuber_____, in fact, that they had to be
   asked to be quiet for the announcements.

5. My brother is always very sure of himself, so he is very

   confid_____. He gained a lot of confid_____ as a camp
   counselor last summer.

6. We walked through the fragr_____ botanical gardens.

   The fragr_____ of the flowers was wonderful.

© Macmillan/McGraw-Hill

 R 1.0 Word Analysis, Fluency, and Systematic Vocabulary Development

Name _____

A. Write each word next to its definition.

vital	conserve	sedated	analyzing
speculated	embedded	dehydrated	propelled

1. examining carefully and in detail in order to understand something _____

2. moved or driven forward _____

3. avoid waste; save or preserve _____

4. of greatest importance _____

5. medicated to calm or go to sleep _____

6. thought of reasons or answers _____

7. dried out due to lost water or moisture _____

8. set into surrounding matter _____

B. Write four sentences using one of the vocabulary words in each sentence.

9. _____

_____

10. _____

_____

11. _____

_____

12. _____

_____

Read the paragraph. Then answer the questions.

The Florida Everglades are home to many birds, reptiles, and mammals. The Everglades provide a variety of habitats. They are vital to the wildlife they support, supplying particular environmental conditions that can be found only in the Everglades. Birds and other animals are protected by the sawgrass prairies. Crocodiles and alligators live together in the swamps and water. People must protect and preserve this land in order to nurture and protect the wildlife that make the Everglades their home.

1. What is the main idea of this paragraph?

   _____

   _____

2. Where is the main idea of this paragraph located?

   _____

3. Why do you think it is located there?

   _____

4. What purpose do the first and second sentences serve?

   _____

5. Why are the Everglades vital to wildlife?

   _____

   _____

 R 2.0 Reading Comprehension (Focus on Informational Materials)

As you read *Interrupted Journey*, fill in the Main Idea Chart.

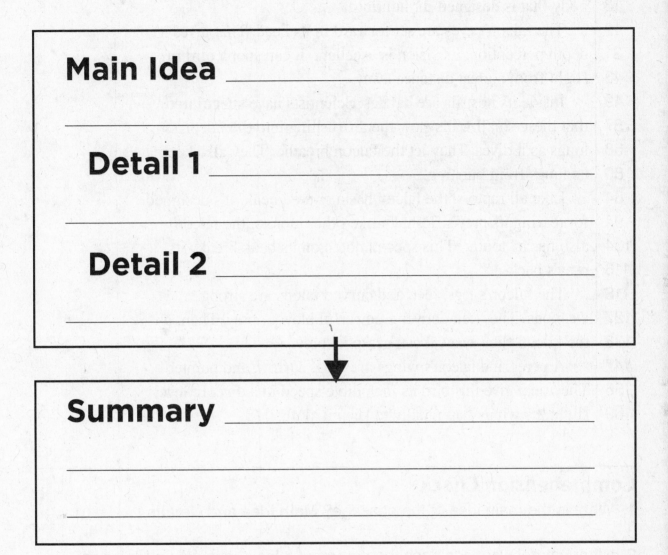

Main Idea _____

_____

Detail 1 _____

_____

Detail 2 _____

_____

Summary _____

_____

_____

How does the information you wrote in this Main Idea Chart help you make inferences and analyze the story structure of *Interrupted Journey*?

As I read, I will pay attention to pacing.

13	The peregrine falcon is a raptor, a bird of prey. It has a body that is designed for hunting.
19	The falcon's eyes are set forward in its head. That gives it
31	depth perception. Its vision is excellent. It can spot a bird in
43	flight from a great distance away.
49	Inside its nostrils are baffles. Scientists have **speculated**
57	that these small walls slow the air rushing into the falcon's
68	lungs as it dives. They let the falcon breathe. They also keep
80	its lungs from bursting.
84	Like all raptors, the falcon has a curved beak. It's designed
94	for tearing its prey's flesh. Unlike other raptors, the falcon
104	also has a "tooth." This special notch on its beak breaks its
116	prey's back.
118	The falcon's legs, feet, and curved talons are strong
127	weapons. They can deliver a powerful blow to prey. Then, as
138	the falcon flies away, it can grasp its prey.
147	A peregrine falcon's wings are long, narrow, and pointed.
156	They help give this bird its incredible speed in a dive. In level
169	flight, its wings flap rapidly to keep it aloft. 178

Comprehension Check

1. What is the main idea of the passage? **Main Idea and Details**

2. What natural weapons does the peregrine falcon have? **Main Idea and Details**

	Words Read	–	Number of Errors	=	Words Correct Score
First Read		–		=	
Second Read		–		=	

R 1.1 Read aloud narrative and expository text fluently and accurately and with appropriate **pacing**, intonation, and expression.

© Macmillan/McGraw-Hill

Name _____

Alliteration is the repetition of consonant sounds.
Imagery is the use of words to create a picture in the reader's mind.
Tone is the feeling a piece of writing creates in the reader.

A. Read the poem. Then answer the questions.

> Drifting down the river,
> I dangle my feet in the icy water.
> Nearly numb from the tips of my toes,
> wide awake,
> I've never felt so alive.

1. What sounds are repeated in the third line? In the fourth line?

_____

_____

2. What imagery does the poem create in your mind? _____

_____

3. How does reading this poem make you feel? _____

_____

**B. Think about a memorable place you have visited. Write your
own poem. Use alliteration and imagery to capture your feelings
about this place.**

_____

_____

_____

_____

_____

_____

© Macmillan/McGraw-Hill

R 3.4 Define how tone or meaning is conveyed in poetry through word
choice, figurative language, sentence structure, line length, punctuation,
rhythm, repetition, and rhyme.

Using **analogies** requires you to understand how words relate to each other.

Analogies are written like this: up : down :: conserve : waste.

They are read like this: "*Up* is to *down* as *conserve* is to *waste*."

One relationship that is often used is opposites, or **antonyms**, as in the example given above.

A. Choose the best word to complete the analogy. Circle the letter of the correct answer.

1. open : closed :: wild : _____

   a. savage   **b.** quiet   **c.** tame   **d.** barbaric

2. advance : retreat :: comedy : _____

   a. tragedy   **b.** music   **c.** jokes   **d.** laughter

3. agree : disagree :: feast : _____

   a. Thanksgiving   **b.** famine   **c.** festival   **d.** hunger

4. remain : leave :: allow : _____

   a. permit   **b.** decide   **c.** request   **d.** prohibit

5. defeat : victory :: lazy : _____

   a. weary   **b.** ambitious   **c.** aggressive   **d.** decent

B. Write three analogies, using antonyms of your own.

6. _____

7. _____

8. _____

CA R 1.0 Word Analysis, Fluency, and Systematic Vocabulary Development

Name _____

Using the Word Study Steps

1. LOOK at the word.

2. SAY the word aloud.

3. STUDY the letters in the word.

4. WRITE the word.

5. CHECK the word.
Did you spell the word right?
If not, go back to step 1.

A. Missing Vowels

Fill in the missing vowels to form spelling words.

1. pr __ s __ d __ nt
2. d __ s __ pp __ __ r __ nc __
3. p __ rs __ st __ nt
4. __ xc __ ll __ nt
5. d __ f __ __ nc __
6. __ xp __ r __ __ nc __
7. c __ nf __ r __ nce
8. __ bs __ rv __ nt
9. __ mp __ rt __ nt
10. v __ __ l __ nc __

11. h __ s __ t __ nt
12. __ v __ d __ nt
13. c __ nst __ nt
14. __ nc __ d __ nt
15. __ nt __ ll __ g __ nt
16. __ cq __ __ __ nt __ nc __
17. p __ rm __ n __ nt
18. n __ __ s __ nc __
19. fr __ gr __ nc __
20. __ cc __ rr __ nc __

B. Write the Words

Use the lines below to practice writing the spelling words.

_____ _____ _____ _____

_____ _____ _____ _____

_____ _____ _____ _____

_____ _____ _____ _____

_____

© Macmillan/McGraw-Hill

LC 1.5 Spell frequently misspelled words correctly (e.g., their, they're, there).

Interrupted Journey
Grade 6/Unit 6
333

Name _____

A. Proofreading Activity

There are five spelling mistakes in the paragraph below. Circle the misspelled words. Write the words correctly on the line below.

Last summer, the town pool passed a rule that no child under twelve could swim without a parent present. They decided to pass this rule following an insident involving a ten-year-old boy who was a newsance to the swimmers and sunbathers. He never caused any vilance, but everyone was annoyed with him. Due to that one boy, the pool board decided to close the pool to everyone under twelve who didn't have a parent to look after him or her. My friends and I decided to stand up for ourselves. We wrote the pool board a letter explaining how emportant the pool was to us and what a great expeeriance it was for us to enjoy the pool with the other residents in our town. I guess our argument was persuasive. Three days after the new rule went into effect, it was overturned.

1. _____   2. _____   3. _____

4. _____   5. _____

B. Writing Activity

Don't you feel great when you stand up for something you believe in? Write a short story about a time when you stood up for something you really wanted and your efforts paid off. Use at least five spelling words.

_____

_____

_____

_____

_____

_____

_____

© Macmillan/McGraw-Hill

 LC 1.5 Spell frequently misspelled words correctly (e.g., *their, they're, there*).

- For adverbs that end in -*ly* and most other adverbs with two or more syllables, use *more* to form the comparative and *most* to form the superlative.
- When you use *more* or *most*, do not use the ending -*er* or -*est*.

A. Write the comparative or superlative forms of each of the following adverbs.

	Comparative	Superlative
1. suddenly	_____	_____
2. frequently	_____	_____
3. widely	_____	_____
4. naturally	_____	_____
5. weakly	_____	_____

B. Each sentence below contains an incorrectly formed adverb in parentheses. Put brackets [ ] around the correct adverb.

6. Andre traveled (most comfortably, more comfortably) in the time machine than Thomas.

7. Andre slept (more soundly, most soundly) of all the boys.

8. Thomas said, "My flashlight shines (most radiantly, radiantlier) of all."

9. Andre sings (more naturally, most naturally) than Thomas.

10. Thomas sang (most forcefully, more forcefully) of all.

- The **comparative** form of an adverb compares two actions.
- The **superlative** form of an adverb compares more than two actions.

Correct any errors in the use of comparative and superlative adverbs, and in the use of *well* and *badly* in the directions below. Then rewrite the explanatory essay, correcting any errors in the use of adverbs, capitalization, or punctuation.

You do not need to reason most brilliantly than Albert Einstein in order to well understand the dimension of time. Many people most incorrectlyest believe that time is a constant, and that we are moving eagerlier through time at a fixed rate. But you can perform a well-known experiment to show that time is not constant. Try sitting through a boring movie. Does time move quicklyer? Then think about a ride on a roller coaster. Does time move fastest then? There is no easy explanation for why time moves more quickly sometimes and more slowly at other times. It's just a fact of life.

_____

_____

_____

_____

_____

_____

_____

_____

_____

_____

 LC 1.0 Written and Oral English Language Conventions

Name _____

Yesterday was such a hilarious day. My brother made me laugh so loud. Our house has mice in it. My brother decided he would scare them. He snuck over to our neighbor's house. I couldn't believe what he did next. Our neighbor has a cat statue outside. He borrowed the neighbor's statue! Then, he walked back to our house. Finally, he ran through the house screaming with the cat statue in his hand.

1. Read the paragraph at the top of the page.

2. Count the number of words in each sentence.

3. Fill in the Sentence Length Chart together. Since there are 6 words in the first sentence, use the chart and fill out the row next to the number 1. Fill in 6 boxes. Now do the same for the rest of the sentences.

4. If you discover that most of the sentences are the same length, consider that it would be good to vary the length of some of the sentences.

5. Look for a spot where changing the length of the sentence might make the piece more interesting. Underline a place where two sentences could be combined.

6. Now combine two sentences and write the new sentence on the line below:

_____

7. Look for any places where you could cut the sentences short. Write those new sentences on the line below.

_____

Sentence Length Chart

		Sentence Length (# of words)										
		1	2	3	4	5	6	7	8	9	10	11+
Sentence Number	1											
	2											
	3											
	4											
	5											
	6											
	7											
	8											
	9											
	10											
	11											
	12											

The Greek suffixes **-logy** and **-ology** mean "the science or the study of" whatever the root or base word indicates. **Biology** is the science of plant and animal life.

The suffix **-ician** means "practitioner, someone who practices or works with" whatever the root or base word indicates. A **musician** is someone who practices or plays music.

The suffix **-crat** means "a person who rules or governs." An **autocrat** is someone who rules all by himself or herself.

Using what you know about Greek suffixes, write a definition of each word listed below. Then use the word in a sentence of your own.

1. politician _____

_____

2. technology _____

_____

3. aristocrat _____

_____

4. ecology _____

_____

_____

5. electrician _____

_____

6. bureaucrat _____

_____

 R 1.0 Word Analysis, Fluency, and Systematic Vocabulary Development

A. Answer the questions about the vocabulary words.

1. What is the difference between a *renewable* and a *nonrenewable* resource?

Give examples of each. _____

_____

_____

2. Name one *adverse* effect that has happened in our environment. _____

_____

_____

3. What does it mean to *generate* electricity? _____

_____

4. What is an *apparatus*? Give an example. _____

_____

_____

B. Write a paragraph about using resources responsibly. Use three of the five vocabulary words: *renewable, nonrenewable, adverse, generate, apparatus.* **Underline the vocabulary words you use.**

_____

_____

_____

_____

_____

_____

_____

_____

Read the paragraph. Then answer the questions.

"Building Green" is one way to conserve natural resources and protect the environment, but it is expensive and requires dedication to change. There are other ways you can conserve energy that will result in reduced pollution, and you don't have to move! One way to conserve energy is to pay attention to the heating and cooling in your home. If you turn the thermostat down in the winter and up in the summer, the result is a significant decrease in the use of electricity or gas. Even changing the temperature a few degrees will save a bundle of energy. Another way to conserve natural resources is to put the car keys away. Cars use gasoline, which comes from a nonrenewable resource. If you can, take a bus or train, ride a bike, or walk. Doing so will help you save money on gasoline, reduce the amount of fossil fuels you use, and help the environment by not burning those fuels. Going green is easier than you think!

1. What is the effect of turning down the heat in the winter?

_____

2. How can you help the environment? _____

_____

_____

3. Name three effects of not driving.

   A. _____

   B. _____

   C. _____

4. Why is "going green" easy to do? _____

_____

_____

_____

© Macmillan/McGraw-Hill

 CA **R 2.0-** Reading Comprehension (Focus on Informational Materials)

As you read *Building Green*, fill in the Cause and Effect Chart.

Cause	→	Effect
	→	
	→	
	→	

How does the information you wrote in this Cause and Effect Chart help you better understand *Building Green*?

As I read, I will pay attention to pronunciation.

	Click on the TV. Turn up the heat. Go for a ride in the car.
15	What do all these actions have in common? They all use
26	energy. Energy is an important part of our lives. Try to
37	imagine going through a day without it. First, take away
47	everything that uses electricity. No refrigerator, no TV, no
56	light bulbs. Then shut down everything that runs on gasoline
66	or fuel. No cars, trucks, planes, or trains. Next, turn off the
78	natural gas or oil that keeps your home warm on bitter cold
90	nights. You get the idea—energy powers our lives.
99	Most of the energy we use comes from fossil fuels—coal,
110	oil, and natural gas. These energy sources are called fossil
120	fuels because they formed from plants and animals that died
130	millions of years ago.
134	Fossil fuels have many uses. Power plants burn coal and
144	oil to generate electricity. Gasoline and fuel for most cars,
154	planes, trains, and ships come from oil. Oil and natural gas
165	provide heat for homes. In many ways, fossil fuels are
175	excellent sources of energy. 179

Comprehension Check

1. What is the main idea of this passage? **Main Idea and Details**

2. What would happen if electricity were taken away? **Draw Conclusions**

	Words Read	−	Number of Errors	=	Words Correct Score
First Read		−		=	
Second Read		−		=	

R 1.1 Read aloud narrative and expository text fluently and accurately and with appropriate pacing, intonation, and expression.

© Macmillan/McGraw-Hill

Name _____

Study strategies are ways that help you learn new material and manage the information you already know.

Skimming—Look over material you have read. Don't read every word. Just look at the headings, boldfaced words, italicized sentences, pictures, and other things that stand out in the text. What do you know about them?

Scanning—If you need specific information about the Revolutionary War, for example, scan the text for key words that relate to the subject. Make a note of pictures, time lines, or other visuals that might have something to do with the topic you are reviewing.

Notetaking—If you haven't already done so, take notes on the most important aspects of the text. Record important terms and dates. Write brief definitions or descriptions to remind you of the knowledge you already have.

Outlining—One way to clearly identify main points is to construct outlines of sections of text. You can use a formal or informal outline. Whatever you choose, be sure to record the main ideas and supporting details in the text.

Choose a chapter or section from your social studies or science book. Skim the text for the most important information. Make an outline of the reading in the space below.

_____

_____

_____

_____

_____

_____

_____

_____

Cause/Effect Writing Frame

Summarize *Building Green*.
A. Use the Cause/Effect Writing Frame below.

Many homes today have a bad effect on the environment. This is **causing** builders to make special "green" homes that are ecologically friendly.

One home in Texas, _____
_____
_____ .

The **effects** of these improvements include _____
_____
_____ .

One home in California, _____
_____
_____ .

The **effects** of these improvements include _____
_____
_____
_____ .

In Arizona, a company is _____
_____
_____ .

The **effects** of this improvement includes _____
_____
_____
_____ .

B. Rewrite the completed summary on another sheet of paper. Keep it as
   a model for writing a summary of an article or selection using this text
   structure.

© Macmillan/McGraw-Hill

 R 2.0 Reading Comprehension (Focus on Informational Materials)

Name _____

> Context refers to the words and sentences that surround an unfamiliar word. **Context clues** come in different forms but are often included within the same sentence as the unfamiliar word. Sometimes the clues will be in the form of definitions, restatements, or synonyms. Other times, the clue will be in a contrasting word. Often the general context will give you an idea about the meaning of the word.

Use the context clues in the sentences to define the underlined words.

1. We need to be <u>economical</u>, not wasteful, with natural resources.

   _____

2. Mining for natural resources often destroys the <u>habitats</u>, or homes, of endangered animals.

   _____

3. If we use fewer <u>fossil fuels</u>, such as oil and coal, that are made from the remains of plants and animals, there will be less demand for them.

   _____

4. If more <u>efficient</u> cars are built, they will use less gasoline and oil to run, and will place less stress on the environment.

   _____

5. <u>Architects</u>, the people who design buildings, are coming up with new ways to save energy every day.

   _____

6. To <u>purify</u>, or clean, the air, people should plant more trees.

   _____

R 1.4 Monitor expository text for unknown words or words with novel meanings by using word, sentence, and paragraph clues to determine meaning.

Name _____

Using the Word Study Steps

1. LOOK at the word.

2. SAY the word aloud.

3. STUDY the letters in the word.

4. WRITE the word.

5. CHECK the word.
Did you spell the word right?
If not, go back to step 1.

ACROSS

1. a piano player

5. a doctor

6. advances in tools and knowledge

7. a person who creates music

DOWN

1. a person who participates in politics

2. a person who visits a place far from their home

3. coded message sent over wires

4. a person who is particularly knowledgeable in a specific field

 LC 1.5 Spell frequently misspelled words correctly (e.g., *their, they're, there*).

© Macmillan/McGraw-Hill

Name _____

A. Proofreading

There are five spelling mistakes in the paragraph below. Circle the misspelled words. Write the words correctly on the lines below.

If there is one profession I most want to be, it is a polititian. I would love to contribute to the democrasy of this country. I imagine it must be hard. I always have simpathy for the candidate who loses, regardless of whether they are a demokrat or a republican. If I became a civil servant, I would hope to demonstrate the herosm that the public really needs.

1. _____   2. _____   3. _____

4. _____   5. _____

B. Writing Activity

What would you like to be when you grow up? Write a short paragraph about the career you would like to pursue, and steps you think you would need to take to obtain it. Use five spelling words.

_____

_____

_____

_____

_____

_____

_____

_____

_____

_____

LC 1.5 Spell frequently misspelled words correctly
(e.g., *their, they're, there*).

Name _____

> You can correct a double **negative** by replacing one negative with
> a positive word.

**Read each sentence. If the sentence contains a double negative, rewrite
it correctly. If the sentence is correct, write C on the line provided.**

1. Lupe decided to ask her grandfather for help, not her grandmother.

_____

_____

2. Lupe's grandfather, Oswaldo, wasn't no easy teacher.

_____

_____

3. But Lupe knew she wouldn't never find a better person to teach her
Spanish.

_____

_____

4. Most grandparents didn't never get the opportunity to teach their
grandchildren.

_____

_____

5. Oswaldo was not going to miss it!

_____

_____

6. Oswaldo wasn't sorry he studied Spanish.

_____

_____

 LC 1.0 Written and Oral English Language Conventions

- A **negative** is a word that means "no," such as *not*, *never*, *nobody*, *nowhere*, and contractions with *n't*.
- A **double negative** is an error in which two negatives are used together.
- You can correct a double negative by removing one negative.
- You can correct a double negative by replacing one negative with a positive word.

Proofread the persuasive editorial below for errors in the use of negatives, punctuation, and capitalization. Then rewrite the editorial.

   As president of the school council, I have been asked to comment on the effort by a group of students to take down the class photos in the corridor outside principal hernandez's Office. These photos show graduates of cleveland middle school for the last twenty five years. The students who don't believe these class photos should not be replaced with decorative posters don't not understand that our past is a part of us. I strongly urge students to keep in touch with the present and future by not preserving our reminders of the past.

_____

_____

_____

_____

_____

_____

_____

_____

_____

_____

Name _____

Writing Rubric

	4 Excellent	3 Good	2 Fair	1 Unsatisfactory
	Ideas and Content/ Genre	Ideas and Content/ Genre	Ideas and Content/ Genre	Ideas and Content/ Genre
	Organization and Focus	Organization and Focus	Organization and Focus	Organization and Focus
	Sentence Structure/ Fluency	Sentence Structure/ Fluency	Sentence Structure/ Fluency	Sentence Structure/ Fluency
	Conventions	Conventions	Conventions	Conventions
	Word Choice	Word Choice	Word Choice	Word Choice
	Voice	Voice	Voice	Voice
	Presentation	Presentation	Presentation	Presentation

© Macmillan/McGraw-Hill

CA W 1.0 Writing Strategies

You can often recognize absorbed prefixes, such as *ac-*, *ar-*, *il-*,
im-, and *ir-*, because the final consonant of the prefix is doubled.
They are prefixes whose spelling changes because they would
be awkward in their original form. Usually, the absorbed prefix is
close to the original prefix, which you may already know.

**A. In the words below, identify the absorbed prefix by underlining
it. Then identify the original prefix from the meaning of the word.**

1. immigrate _____

2. accompany _____

3. announce _____

4. arrive _____

5. illogical _____

6. irregular _____

7. illuminate _____

8. immature _____

9. arrest _____

10. illegal _____

B. Write sentences of your own using two of the words listed above.

11. _____

_____

12. _____

_____

Answer each question about a vocabulary word.

outskirts	quarantine	intercept	pedestrians
plight	epidemic	rendezvous	unbearable

1. Where would you be likely to find **pedestrians**? _____

_____

2. Name something that you find **unbearable**. _____

_____

3. What is a synonym for **rendezvous**? _____

_____

4. Where are the **outskirts** of town? _____

_____

5. What kinds of things can you **intercept**? Give two examples. _____

_____

6. If something happens in **epidemic** proportions, how does it happen?

_____

_____

7. Describe in general the **plight** of endangered species. _____

_____

_____

8. When would you need to **quarantine** an animal? _____

_____

_____

CA R 1.0 Word Analysis, Fluency, and Systematic Vocabulary Development

Name _____

Read the summary of the story "The King of Mazy May," by Jack London.

Walt Masters is the main character of "The King of Mazy May," by Jack London. When Walt was little, his mother died. He and his father moved to the Klondike, a region in Alaska known for its gold. They were prospectors, or people who looked for gold. At the time, prospectors had to make their claims on land quickly or claim jumpers would try to steal the land. Walt, though still a boy, was given the job of protecting his neighbor Loren's claim while Loren traveled on foot to make his claim to the land official.

Walt noticed some strangers who were claim jumpers. He spied on them. He learned that they hoped to get to Dawson to stake the claims before anyone else could. Walt knew he had to do something. He took a team of the claim jumpers' dogs and raced to Dawson. The men followed him closely and actually shot at him. Without the dogs, Walt would have been an easy target. But those dogs saved his life. Not only that, they saved Loren's claim in the end.

A. Number each event in the order that it happened in the story.

_____ Walt helped Loren save his claim to the land.

_____ Walt and his father moved to the Klondike.

_____ Walt saw some claim jumpers in the area.

_____ Walt's mother died.

_____ Walt took the claim jumpers' dogs and headed for Dawson.

_____ Walt was given the job of protecting his neighbor's claim.

B. What is your opinion of how Walt acted? On the lines below, write a brief paragraph explaining how you feel about what Walt did.

_____

_____

_____

_____

Name _____

As you read *The Great Serum Race*, fill in the Sequence Chart.

```
┌─────────────────────────────────────────────┐
│                                               │
│                   Event                       │
│                                               │
└─────────────────────────────────────────────┘
                        │
                        ▼
┌─────────────────────────────────────────────┐
│                                               │
│                                               │
│                                               │
└─────────────────────────────────────────────┘
                        │
                        ▼
┌─────────────────────────────────────────────┐
│                                               │
│                                               │
│                                               │
└─────────────────────────────────────────────┘
                        │
                        ▼
┌─────────────────────────────────────────────┐
│                                               │
│                                               │
│                                               │
└─────────────────────────────────────────────┘
                        │
                        ▼
┌─────────────────────────────────────────────┐
│                                               │
│                                               │
│                                               │
└─────────────────────────────────────────────┘
```

How does the information you wrote in this Sequence Chart help you
better understand *The Great Serum Race*?

R 2.0 Reading Comprehension (Focus on Informational Materials)

Name _____

As I read, I will pay attention to the pronunciation of vocabulary and other difficult words.

	On the **outskirts** of Anchorage, Alaska, 12 dogs jump and
9	bark. They have been training for months. Now these furry
19	athletes and their human driver, or musher, are about to set off on
32	an amazing journey. They're going to race the Iditarod. They'll
42	run more than 1,100 miles up snow-covered mountains, through
50	blizzards, and across frozen tundra and jagged ice sheets.
59	Temperatures may fall to minus 50 degrees Fahrenheit (-45° Celsius).
67	Most animals couldn't hope to survive such dangerous conditions.
76	But these dogs can't wait to begin! They are Alaskan huskies, bred
88	for this weather and this job. They love to run through the icy
101	North.
102	In the late 1800s and early 1900s, many people who lived in
112	Alaska depended on sled dogs. They lived far from transportation.
122	Winters there were harsh. The best way to get around was to use
135	sled dogs. Over the years, the dogs saved many lives. They helped
147	people keep in touch with each other and the outside world.
158	Without the dogs, life might have been **unbearable** for some of
169	the settlers. 171

Comprehension Check

1. What conditions might a sled dog face? **Summarize**

2. What problems did people have in the late 1800s in Alaska? How did dogs help? **Problem and Solution**

	Words Read	−	Number of Errors	=	Words Correct Score
First Read		−		=	
Second Read		−		=	

R 1.1 Read aloud narrative and expository text fluently and accurately and with appropriate pacing, intonation, and expression.

© Macmillan/McGraw-Hill

Name _____

Haiku is an unrhymed form of Japanese poetry that is usually
three lines long.

The first line in Haiku has five syllables; the second line, seven;
the third, five. Haiku often describes something in nature.

Symbolism is the use of an everyday object to stand for
something more meaningful.

Metaphor is a comparison of two essentially unlike things.

**Try your hand at writing haiku. Write three poems that picture
different seasons. In at least one poem, include a symbol. For
example, flower buds can symbolize the coming of spring.
Use a metaphor in at least one poem.**

When you finish, you may draw a picture for each haiku.

_____

_____

_____

_____

_____

_____

_____

_____

 R 3.4 Define how tone or meaning is conveyed in poetry through
word choice, **figurative language**, sentence structure, line length,
punctuation, rhythm, repetition, and rhyme.

Synonyms are words that have the same or nearly the same meaning. You can use synonyms to help you determine the meaning of unfamiliar words. Often, synonyms are used as context clues.

Example: Jennie was scheduled to intercept, or seize, the message at midnight.
The word *seize* is a synonym for *intercept*.

A. Use a dictionary or thesaurus to find a synonym for each of the following words.

1. majestic _____

2. hospitable _____

3. dejected _____

4. abbreviated _____

5. reasonable _____

B. Choose two sets of synonyms from the list above and write a paragraph that includes them.

6. _____

_____

_____

_____

_____

_____

_____

_____

Using the Word Study Steps

1. LOOK at the word.
2. SAY the word aloud.
3. STUDY the letters in the word.
4. WRITE the word.
5. CHECK the word.
   Did you spell the word right?
   If not, go back to step 1.

Find the Words

Find and circle the spelling words in the puzzle below.

```
I  L  L  O  G  I  C  A  L  A  C  C  O  M
D  A  S  S  E  M  B  L  Y  F  P  E  G  R
R  I  U  P  I  M  A  N  N  O  U  N  C  E
I  M  P  A  T  I  E  N  T  L  Y  A  C  I
M  M  P  C  O  G  A  H  A  J  I  G  O  L
M  A  R  C  A  R  R  E  S  T  L  I  L  L
I  T  E  O  B  A  R  R  U  S  L  R  L  U
G  U  S  M  C  T  I  X  P  A  E  R  A  M
R  R  S  P  O  E  V  P  P  R  G  E  B  I
A  E  H  A  L  H  E  N  O  A  A  G  O  N
T  P  R  N  L  L  D  S  R  E  L  U  R  A
I  D  E  Y  E  I  H  I  T  H  K  L  A  T
O  N  M  A  C  C  O  M  M  O  D  A  T  E
N  I  X  H  T  S  U  F  F  I  X  R  E  C
C  O  R  R  E  S  P  O  N  D  L  E  K  Y
```

 LC 1.5 Spell frequently misspelled words correctly
(e.g., *their, they're, there*).

© Macmillan/McGraw-Hill

A. Proofreading

There are five spelling mistakes in the paragraph below. Circle the misspelled words. Write the words correctly on the lines below.

Salvatore often imagined what it would be like to travel to another time. His family had moved from Italy to New York when he was ten. He imagined that living in another century would be similar to how he felt when his family decided to emmigrate. He supposed the immigrasion process would be much more difficult if you traveled back in time to the eighteenth century. Salvatore guessed that if he were to arive back then things would seem more irreguler and ilogical than when he moved from Italy.

1. _____   2. _____   3. _____

4. _____   5. _____

B. Writing Activity

Did you ever fantasize about time travel? Imagine that you have traveled back in time. Write a letter to a friend describing your experience. Use at least five spelling words.

_____

_____

_____

_____

_____

_____

_____

_____

_____

_____

_____

CA LC 1.5 Spell frequently misspelled words correctly
(e.g., *their, they're, there*).

The Great Serum Race   359
Grade 6/Unit 6

- A **prepositional phrase** is a group of words that begins with a **preposition** and ends with a noun or pronoun.
- The object of a preposition is the noun or pronoun that follows the preposition.
- The verb must agree with the subject, not with the object of the preposition.

A. Read each sentence below. Underline each prepositional phrase, and put brackets [ ] around the object of the preposition. One sentence has two prepositional phrases.

1. Ashley found herself becoming interested in the newspaper business.

2. She asked her teacher to recommend books about journalism.

3. Ashley's teacher gave her a list with several titles.

4. Ashley selected one of the books from the school library.

5. She put the book into her backpack.

B. Each sentence below contains a correct and an incorrect verb in parentheses. Put brackets [ ] around the correct verb. Then, on the line below each sentence, rewrite the sentence without the prepositional phrase.

6. The book in the backpack (belongs, belong) to Ashley.

_____

7. The book in the backseat of the car (needs, need) to be returned.

_____

8. The rules of the library (is, are) important.

_____

9. Ashley's neighbors across the street (were, was) journalists.

_____

10. Their articles in the newspaper (was, were) fascinating.

_____

© Macmillan/McGraw-Hill

 LC 1.0 Written and Oral English Language Conventions

Name _____

- A **preposition** comes before a noun or pronoun and relates that noun or pronoun to another word in the sentence.
- Common prepositions are *about, above, across, after, around, at, before, behind, below, between, down, for, from, in, near, of, on, over, to,* and *with*.
- A **prepositional phrase** is a group of words that begins with a preposition and ends with a noun or pronoun.
- The object of a preposition is the noun or pronoun that follows the preposition.
- The verb must agree with the subject, not with the object of the preposition.

Read the following explanation of a process. Correct any mistakes in the use of prepositions, prepositional phrases, capitalization, and punctuation. Then rewrite the explanation.

The process of writing and publishing a book have changed dramatically in the last 15 years. Before the advent of computers, writers needed publishing companies to print bind and distribute their books. Now it can all be done electronically. First, write your story. Then read through your rough draft which is also called a first pass. When you are sure your story is as good as it can be create your own Web site and become your own publisher!

_____

_____

_____

_____

_____

_____

_____

_____

_____

_____

Name _____

1. Read the following sentence:

   During homeroom, Richard collected the forms, and Giovanni wrote the date on the board.

2. Circle the two subjects of the COMPOUND sentence. (Note that a compound sentence contains two complete sentences connected by a conjunction.)

3. Read the following sentence:

   Amy hit the high note, but Carol played the wrong note during rehearsal.

4. Underline the two predicates of the COMPOUND sentence. (Note that a compound sentence contains two complete sentences connected by a conjunction.)

5. Read the following sentence:

   The trees looked awfully brown, and the grass wasn't growing after more than 13 months of drought.

6. Circle the two subjects, and underline the two predicates of the COMPOUND sentence. (Note that a compound sentence contains two complete sentences connected by a conjunction.)

7. Now, turn to your journal entry on being part of an unsuccessful team. (If you do not have that entry, go to the most recent entry.)

8. Write TWO compound sentences below that you could add to your journal entry. (Remember that you are not necessarily trying to make the journal entry better. You are using the entry to practice writing compound sentences. But you never know—maybe you'll write something you can use!)

   _____

   _____

   _____

   _____

   _____

© Macmillan/McGraw-Hill

9. Read over your sentences. Circle the subjects and write *S* above them. Underline the predicates and write *P* above them.

 CA W 1.0 Writing Strategies

Name _____

Many words in English come from Greek and Roman **mythology**. The gods and goddesses of these early myths had certain characteristics that are reflected in the modern words formed from their names. An example of a word taken from mythology is *cereal*. This word is from *Ceres*, the Roman goddess of agriculture, because *cereal* is made from grain.

Study the words in the chart that are taken from Greek or Roman mythology. Choose five of the words and use each in a sentence of your own. Underline the words in your sentences.

Word	Word from Mythology
east	Eos: Greek goddess of the dawn
flower	Flora: Roman goddess of flowers
martial	Mars: Roman god of war
panic	Pan: Greek god of shepherds
jovial	Jupiter: Most powerful Roman god
volcano	Vulcan: Roman god of fire
Saturday	Saturn: Roman god of agriculture
January	Janus: Roman god of beginnings
May	Maia: Roman goddess of growth

1. _____

2. _____

3. _____

4. _____

5. _____

_____

© Macmillan/McGraw-Hill

Name _____

Use the clues to complete the crossword.

flee   exterior   structures   residents
exhaustion volunteered   perished   consumed

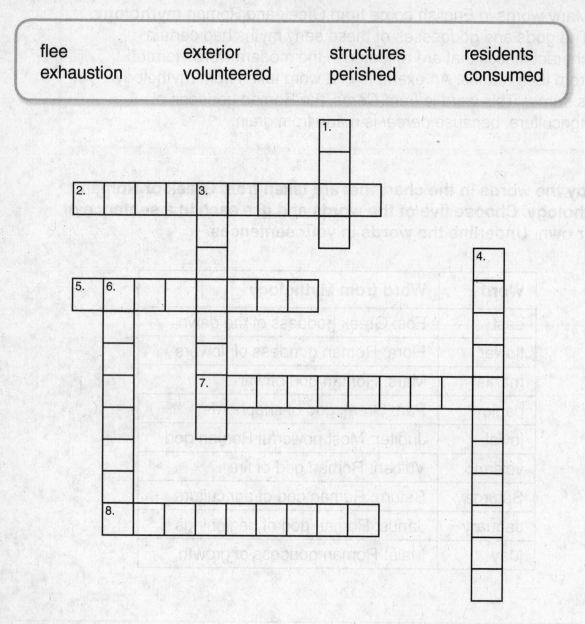

Across

2. buildings
5. died
7. the state of being extremely tired
8. people who live in a particular place

Down

1. run away
3. used up or destroyed
4. offered one's services without pay
6. the outside of something

 R 1.0 Word Analysis, Fluency, and Systematic Vocabulary Development

In stories and in real life, one event can make another event occur. For example, if you forget your umbrella on a rainy day, then you will get wet. The first event is the **cause**, and the second event is the **effect**. Authors use **signal words** or **phrases** such as *as a result*, *so*, *therefore*, *because*, *due to*, and *then* to show cause-and-effect relationships between events.

Read the following paragraph. Underline the signal words or phrases that show the relationships between events. Then write the cause and effect of each situation as indicated by the signal words.

In 1906, a disastrous fire occurred in San Francisco due to a powerful earthquake. The fire began because stoves and lamps were toppled by the tremors in the earth. The fire destroyed the city's water mains. Therefore, it was impossible for firefighters to contain the blaze. San Francisco burned for three days. As a result, nearly 3,000 people lost their lives.

1. cause _____

   effect _____

2. cause _____

   effect _____

3. cause _____

   effect _____

   _____

4. cause _____

   effect _____

Name _____

As you read *The Great Fire*, fill in the Cause and Effect Chart.

Cause	→	Effect
	→	
	→	
	→	
	→	
	→	
	→	
	→	

© Macmillan/McGraw-Hill

How does the Cause and Effect Chart help you analyze the text structure of
The Great Fire?

 R 2.0 Reading Comprehension (Focus on Informational Materials)

As I read, I will pay attention to intonation and pacing.

	When I was in sixth grade, my friends were doing amazing things.
12	Ann wrote beautiful poems. Ray drew funny cartoons. Donna was
22	a sports nut. She played soccer and basketball, and was a star on the
36	swim team. Heather went to every new movie and had strong feelings
48	about each one.
51	I felt privileged to have such interesting friends. I was so proud of
64	them that I wanted to tell the world. So I started a newspaper. Every
78	month I collected interesting stories and articles by and about the other
90	sixth-grade kids at Humiston School.
95	I named the newspaper the *Scribe*. It was printed on a photocopy
107	machine. I sold each copy for five cents, and every issue sold out.
120	I knew that I loved working on the *Scribe*, and I knew that my friends
135	liked reading it. What I didn't know was that I was a publisher.
148	The publisher is the person who takes a writer's manuscript and
159	turns it into a book or an article for a magazine or newspaper.
172	Sometimes you read something you like. You're curious about the
182	writer. But you probably don't wonder about the publisher. That's
192	because the publisher's work happens behind the scenes. But even if
203	you aren't aware of the publisher's job, it's still important. 213

Comprehension Check

1. How would you describe the author's group of friends? **Description**

2. How did the author publish the newspaper? **Summarize**

	Words Read	–	Number of Errors	=	Words Correct Score
First Read		–		=	
Second Read		–		=	

R 1.1 Read aloud narrative and expository text fluently and accurately
and with appropriate pacing, intonation, and expression.

A primary source is information that comes from the time being studied. It could be a newspaper or magazine article, letters, photographs, or an official document.

A. Read the following entries. One is a primary source and the other is not. Write a P on the space provided if you think the entry is a Primary Source.

1. _____ "I was awakened by a loud rumbling sound. The bed began to shake. Cans and boxes toppled off the kitchen shelves. My clock fell off the wall and crashed to the floor."

2. _____ Although he was just a boy at the time, my grandfather remembers the fire as if it were yesterday. He often tells me how his family and all their neighbors threw buckets of water on the blazing barn. He describes the red and orange flames that rose taller than the silo.

B. Explain how you decided which entry was a primary source and which one was not.

_____

_____

_____

_____

_____

_____

_____

_____

_____

_____

 R 2.1 Identify structural features of popular media (e.g., newspapers, magazines, online information) and use the features to obtain information.

Name _____

Read the paragraph. Answer the questions.

One of the most important things to remember when calamity strikes is not to panic. A panicky person cannot think clearly. A person who panics cannot maneuver through the obstacles presented by a disaster, such as a tornado or hurricane. Each kind of disaster requires a different action. For example, a tornado requires people to go to the center of a building, preferably a room with no windows, or a basement, and cover their heads. A hurricane, on the other hand, requires evacuation because the storm surge can flood areas. If the storm surge rises too high, people will be stranded on rooftops and unable to get to safety. In the event of an earthquake, people should get outside or stand in doorways for protection. Seismic activity causes the ground to shake and buildings to come toppling down in some cases. Regardless of the kind of natural disaster, a calm approach will allow you to think things through and act appropriately for the situation.

1. What does *maneuver* mean? _____

_____

2. Which clues helped you define *maneuver*? _____

_____

_____

3. What is a storm surge? _____

_____

4. Which clues helped you define *storm surge*? _____

_____

_____

5. What is seismic activity? _____

6. Which clues helped you define *seismic activity*? _____

_____

_____

R 1.4 Monitor expository text for unknown words or words with
novel meanings by using word, sentence, and paragraph clues to
determine meaning.

Name _____

Using the Word Study Steps

1. LOOK at the word.
2. SAY the word aloud.
3. STUDY the letters in the word.
4. WRITE the word.
5. CHECK the word.
   Did you spell the word right?
   If not, go back to step 1.

A. Missing Letters

Fill in the missing letters to form spelling words.

1. _____ metry
2. hyg _____
3. ter _____
4. _____ tar
5. _____ ology
6. ch _____ s
7. mara _____
8. ir _____
9. ti _____ ic
10. tanta _____

11. cos _____ ics
12. geo _____ y
13. mer _____
14. _____ urnal
15. ro _____ ce
16. m _____ ia
17. so _____
18. _____ bia
19. _____ sia
20. heli _____ ter

B. Write the Words

Use the lines below to practice writing the spelling words.

_____ _____ _____ _____

_____ _____ _____ _____

_____ _____ _____ _____

_____ _____ _____ _____

© Macmillan/McGraw-Hill

 LC 1.5 Spell frequently misspelled words correctly
(e.g., *their, they're, there*).

Name _____

A. There are five spelling mistakes in the paragraph below. Circle the misspelled words. Write the words correctly on the lines below.

Mr. Casey asked his students to write essays on what they felt has been the greatest invention of all time. Hakeem wrote about the helicoptar, even though he had never been in one. Sharon wrote about cosmetiks, even though her mother wouldn't let her wear any. Petra felt that advances in personal hygeene were important, but she had a germ phobea. Mr. Casey found many of the class's essays tanttalizzing, but claimed that the printing press was the most important invention because without it, we wouldn't have books or the ability to share ideas.

1. _____   2. _____   3. _____

4. _____   5. _____

B. Writing Activity

What do you think is the most important contribution to modern society? Write a paragraph describing something you think is essential to the way we live. Use five spelling words.

_____

_____

_____

_____

_____

_____

_____

_____

_____

_____

LC 1.5 Spell frequently misspelled words correctly
(e.g., *their, they're, there*).

> • Two sentences can be combined by adding a prepositional phrase from one sentence to the other.

Read each pair of sentences. Combine the two sentences into one sentence by adding a prepositional phrase. Write the new sentence on the line provided.

1. Regina is a scientist. She works at the University of Rome.

_____

_____

2. Regina works in a special department. The department was specifically formed for studying volcanic activity.

_____

_____

3. Italy's most famous volcano is Vesuvius. It is now dormant.

_____

_____

4. Mount Etna is still erupting. It spews red-hot lava on the eastern coast of Sicily.

_____

_____

5. The land around Mount Etna is very fertile. It is fertile because of the rich soil.

_____

_____

© Macmillan/McGraw-Hill

LC 1.1 Use simple, compound, and compound-complex sentences; use effective coordination and subordination of ideas to express complete thoughts.

- Two sentences can be combined by adding an adjective or adverb from one sentence to the other.
- Two sentences can be combined by adding a prepositional phrase from one sentence to the other.

Combine any sentences you can in the explanation below. Then rewrite the explanation, correcting any mistakes in punctuation, capitalization, or comma usage.

How to Make a Volcano at Home

    In order to make a volcano at home you need baking soda. You need vinegar. You need a container to put your volcano in. Put some baking soda in the container pour in some vinegar. Watch what happens this "eruption" is called an acid base reaction. Your "volcano" really erupts! The eruption is caused by carbon dioxide. The carbon dioxide is given off as the acid in the vinegar neutralizes the sodium bicarbonate in the baking soda.

_____

_____

_____

_____

_____

_____

_____

_____

_____

_____

LC 1.1 Use simple, compound, and compound-complex sentences; use effective coordination and subordination of ideas to express complete thoughts.

Name _____

1. Read the following sentence:

   Bob walks.

2. Circle the subject and underline the predicate.

3. Read the following sentence:

   Bob, one of the tallest people in the world and the star of his local
   basketball team, walks to work.

4. Circle the subject and underline the predicate.

5. Notice that *Bob* is still the simple subject. We have more information about
   Bob, though that is included in the subject.

6. For each of the sentences below:

   Circle the complete subject and write an *s* over it.

   Circle the complete predicate and put a *p* over it.

   Rewrite each sentence by reordering the components.

Note: The new sentence is not always a "better" sentence. It's just different.

   Fried chicken, corned beef, and scrambled eggs—especially when
   they're mixed up with hot sauce and onions—are my favorite foods.

Reorder:

   When flowers bloom in the springtime and the buds begin to open,
   I get happy.

Reorder:

   Yesterday, one of the worst days of my life, I accidentally whacked my
   thumb with a hammer.

Reorder:

   Although brown paper bags aren't that strong, they work pretty well for
   recycling newspapers.

Reorder:

   Fifteen times I've told my little brother not to touch my school books.

Reorder:

© Macmillan/McGraw-Hill

CA **W 1.0** Writing Strategies